About the author

MARY NORWAK was born in London in
1929 and now lives in Essex with her
three children. She has been a journalist
for over twenty years, contributing articles
on food to such publications as *The Times,
The Guardian, The Daily Express, House
and Garden, The Lady* and many others
besides. She is Cookery Editor of *Farmer's
Weekly* and *Freeze*. She is the author of
several books on deep freezing and
cooking, six of which are available from
Sphere Books.

MARY NORWAK's Book on

Jams, Marmalades and Sweet Preserves

SPHERE BOOKS LIMITED
30/32 Gray's Inn Road, London WC1X 8JL

First published in Great Britain in 1973 by Sphere Books Ltd
Copyright © Mary Norwak 1973

Set in Monotype Baskerville

Printed in Great Britain by
Hazell Watson & Viney Ltd
Aylesbury, Bucks

ISBN 0 7221 6443 2

Contents

INTRODUCTION

Writing this book has been a great pleasure. It has been good to turn away from this world of processed and packaged foods, of instant meals and hurried snacks, to the more leisurely life of earlier years. It has been fun to browse through old books, faded newspaper cuttings and family notes, finding favourite stillroom recipes which sometimes involved many days of preparation.

In recent years, women have shied away from the cooking skills which produced delicious (but fattening) results. The freezer has been used to process fruit for winter storage swiftly and safely, and jam-making has suffered a decline. There has even been less interest in the twin pleasures of breakfast and teatime with their essential pots of tempting preserves.

Now there is a gradual movement back to the country way of life and natural foods. There is a renewed interest in the growing of fruit and vegetables, and a revival in the preparation of home produce in old-fashioned ways. We can once again combine economy and flavour in the treasures of the traditional stillroom kept by every good housewife. We can relax in the leisurely preparation of good fruit, making homely jars of jam for tea, gleaming bowls of refreshing marmalade for breakfast, sparkling jellies to use with puddings and ices. Friends can be sure of lovingly-prepared kitchen presents, and we can feel the glow of satisfaction which comes from well-filled shelves of shining, neatly-labelled jam jars.

CHAPTER ONE
Equipment, Ingredients and Methods

The making of jams, jellies and marmalades is not difficult, but it is wise to study a few general rules to get perfect results. Equipment and ingredients need not be expensive, but careful preparation will produce excellent and delicious preserves.

Equipment

A strong preserving pan is a useful piece of equipment if much preserving is planned. This should be of a good size so that the jam can be boiled rapidly without boiling over. The pan should be wide to allow rapid evaporation of liquid to aid setting. A pan should be of copper or aluminium; enamel which is chipped can be dangerous, and zinc or iron spoil colour and flavour. Copper will help to keep green fruits green, but can spoil the colour of red fruit. A large saucepan can be used.

A long-handled wooden spoon enables the jam to be stirred without hot splashes on the hands.

Jam jars can be saved from year to year. Screwtop honey jars and preserving jars can also be used. Thick decorative small glasses can be used for special jellies, fruit butters or cheeses.

A jug made of metal or heatproof glass enables jam to be poured into jars easily.

A sugar thermometer is not essential but takes the guesswork out of many cooking processes.

A jelly bag can be purchased or made from muslin. It can be used suspended between the four legs of an upturned chair. Extra pieces of muslin are useful for tying up pips and pith in marmalade making, and whole spices for some jams.

Wax discs, transparent covers and labels are essential for keeping the jam well and for presenting a neat appearance. They can be bought in packets at stationers, chemists and grocers. Tight-fitting plastic covers can also be used.

Scales should be used for weighing ingredients, which should be measured carefully for the best results.

Fruit

Fruit should be fresh and sound, and not mushy. It should be slightly under-ripe, as very ripe fruit has reduced sugar content, and will affect the setting and keeping quality of the jam. The fruit should be sorted carefully, and any bruised or damaged pieces discarded. Fruit should be gently washed in a sieve or colander, but not immersed in water. The fruit should be dried on absorbent kitchen paper or a cloth before cooking. Fruit should never be washed in hot water, and fruits which are low in pectin, such as strawberries, should be washed as little as possible. Fruit should be stoned or peeled where necessary with stainless steel or silver. These preparations should be made immediately before cooking, or the fruit will deteriorate.

Acid

Acid in the form of lemon juice, citric or tartaric acid, or redcurrant or gooseberry juice is added to some fruits before cooking, to extract pectin, improve colour and prevent crystallisation. It should be added to any fruit with a low acid content, and to any vegetable jam. To 4 lb fruit, allow 2 tablespoons lemon juice *or* ½ teaspoon citric or tartaric acid *or* ¼ pint redcurrant or gooseberry juice.

Pectin

The setting property of jam depends on its pectin content. Fruit falls into three groups according to pectin contained:

Good Pectin Content
Cooking Apples
Blackcurrants

Damsons
Gooseberries
Plums
Quinces
Redcurrants

Medium Pectin Content

Fresh Apricots
Early Blackberries
Greengages
Loganberries

Poor Pectin Content

Late Blackberries
Cherries
Elderberries
Marrows
Medlars
Pears
Rhubarb
Strawberries
Tomatoes

Commercial pectin may be used for jam-making (see Chapter Six, JAMS, JELLIES AND MARMALADES MADE WITH COMMERCIAL PECTIN). Home-made pectin can be made by simmering unpeeled sliced apples, gooseberries or redcurrants in an equal volume of water for 25 minutes, mashing the fruit. The juice should then be strained through a jelly bag and used, or sterilised in preserving jars at boiling point for 5 minutes.

The pectin content of juice can be tested. 1 teaspoon of the cooked fruit juice should be removed from the pan and cooled in a glass. 3 teaspoons of methylated spirit should then be shaken with the juice. If a clear jelly-like clot forms, there is plenty of pectin. Several small clots indicate a medium pectin content. If no clot forms, the pectin content is poor, and 2–4 fluid oz pectin should be added to each lb fruit.

Sugar

Special preserving sugar is best for jam, but loaf or granulated sugar can be used. *Brown sugar* gives a delicious flavour, but not a good set. It can be used in the proportion of one-quarter brown to white sugar. *Honey* also gives a good flavour but prevents firm setting. It can be used in the proportion of one-quarter or one-half honey to sugar. *Golden syrup* has a special flavour but affects setting; it can be used in the same proportions as honey with sugar.

Sugar must always be stirred carefully into the fruit mixture until it has dissolved. If sugar crystals remain undissolved, they may burn on the bottom of the pan and also affect the smoothness of the jam. If sugar is warmed slightly before adding to the fruit, it will dissolve more quickly.

Preparing the Jam

It is important to be methodical in jam-making, as in other successful cookery. All equipment and ingredients should be assembled before cooking is started. Recipes should be carefully followed, since low-pectin fruits need more fruit than sugar, while high-pectin fruits need more sugar than fruit.

Fruit must be cooked slowly to extract pectin, soften skins before adding sugar, and to keep a good colour. Once the sugar has been stirred in and dissolved, it must be boiled rapidly without stirring. This gives a higher yield, better flavour and colour.

The jam must be tested for setting, skimmed, and poured into warm jars, filled to the brim. Wax circles should be put on to the hot jam, and covers put on when the jam is hot or completely cold. The jam should then be labelled and dated, and stored carefully.

Setting Tests

A keeping jam should have 60 per cent added sugar content or three parts sugar to five parts jam. Some jams are ready for setting after only 5 minutes boiling; others take 10–15 minutes, and a few take longer. A setting test should be made early, as some fruits lose their setting qualities if jam is boiled too long and the jam will never set. When the jam reaches setting point, remove it from heat at once.

Temperature Test

Dip a sugar thermometer in hot water. Stir the jam and submerge the thermometer bulb completely in the jam. When it registers 220°–221°F, the jam is cooked.

Weight Test

Weigh the pan and spoon before cooking begins. When the jam weighs 10 lb for every 6 lb of sugar used, the jam is ready. To work out the final correct weight, multiply the quantity of sugar used by ten and divide by six.

Flake Test

Dip a clean wooden spoon in the boiling jam. Let the cooling jam drop from the spoon, and if the drops run together and form a flake, the jam is ready.

Plate Test

Put a little jam on an old plate or saucer and leave it to become cold. If the jam forms a skin and wrinkles when pushed with a spoon or finger, it is ready. The jam pan should be taken off the heat while the test jam is cooling.

Filling & Covering Jars

The finished jam sould be skimmed, preferably with a perforated metal spoon. A knob of butter in the jam will prevent scumming, but will affect the clarity of the jam. Jam with whole fruit or peel should be left to cool in the pan for 10 minutes, before stirring gently to prevent fruit rising in the jars. Pour jam into the jars with a jug (a wide funnel will ensure clean jars) and fill right to the top. Partly-filled jars allow evaporation and fermentation. Tap jar to bring air bubbles to the surface. Cover at once with waxed discs. Cover with transparent covers while hot, or when completely cold. A foil covering will prevent mouse damage if this is likely, or fitted plastic or screw tops can be used. Labels should be fixed neatly, and include the variety of jam and the date of making. Jam should be stored in a cool, dark, dry place.

Yield

It is difficult to quote an exact yield in jam-making, as circumstances of cooking the fruit and final boiling may vary so much. From 1 lb sugar, the yield will be somewhat less than 2 lb jam, and it is best to calculate $1\frac{2}{3}$ lb jam for each lb sugar as an ideal yield. Jams using commercial pectin will give a higher yield; conserves of fruit in thick syrup will also give a slightly higher yield.

Jam-Making Faults

Careful preparation should produce perfect results, but sometimes mistakes occur, and it is useful to know of possible problems.

Mouldy jam results from damp fruit, insufficient boiling, poor storage, badly-filled or covered jars.

Crystallised jam indicates too much sugar in proportion to fruit *or* overcooking jam to stiffen it when too little sugar has been used. Over-cooking and poor stirring resulting in undissolved sugar can also cause the problem.

Fermenting, 'winey' jam results from over-ripe fruit, insufficient sugar or boiling, poor covering and bad storage.

Hard, dry jam results from over-boiling or bad covering when jam is stored in a warm place. Plastic or screwtops will help to prevent this problem.

Syrupy jam or jelly results from lack of pectin, from insufficient boiling, or over-boiling past setting point. Jelly can be affected if strained fruit juice is left too long before cooking.

Poor flavour results from over- or under-ripe fruit, too much sugar, too-slow boiling or over-boiling.

Poor colour results from poor quality fruit, from a poor quality preserving pan, or from storing in a bright light. It can also arise if the fruit is not cooked slowly enough to soften it completely, if the jam is overboiled, or boiled too slowly to setting point.

Cloudy jelly results from poorly strained juice through a bag which is too thin, or if pulp is forced through the bag instead of letting the jelly drip by itself.

CHAPTER TWO
Basic Seasonal Jam Chart

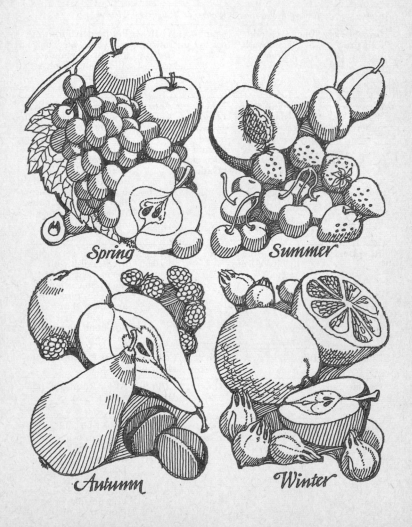

Spring

Summer

Autumn

Winter

This quick reference chart gives basic quantities and methods for the favourite jams usually made in the glut seasons of the respective fruits. Only sound fruit should be used to make good jam. Water should be kept to the minimum, and sugar should preferably be warmed before adding to the cooked fruit to give a shorter boiling time and a richer fruit flavour.

Fruit	Season	Preparation	Water	Sugar	Method
Gooseberry fully grown but unripe	June	Top and tail, wash, drain	½ pint per lb fruit	1½ lb per lb fruit and water	Put prepared fruit in pan with water, boil and stir 20 minutes. Add sugar, dissolve. Boil again 5 to 10 minutes. Pot and cover.
Strawberry slightly under-ripe	Late June early July	Hull fruit and crush slightly	None. Lemon, gooseberry or redcurrant juice may be added	14 oz per lb fruit	Place fruit in pan over gentle heat; crush with back of wooden spoon. Add juice of ½ lemon to each lb strawberries. Stir occasionally while coming to boil, constantly when boiling. Add warmed sugar. Boil about 20 minutes. Allow to cool a few minutes and stir before potting.
Raspberry	July	Remove bits of leaf etc.	None	1 lb per lb fruit	Make fruit very hot (in oven), crush with spoon, beat in hot sugar. Smear butter over pan, turn in fruit and sugar, bring to boil, boil very fast 6 to 8 minutes. Pot and cover at once.
Loganberry	July	Sort over	None	1 lb per lb fruit	As for Raspberry Jam
Redcurrant	July	Stalk, rinse and drain well	None	1 lb per lb fruit	As for Raspberry Jam
Black-currant	July	Stalk and rinse	½ pint per lb fruit	1½ lb per lb fruit and water	Place fruit and water in a pan, bring slowly to boil, crushing fruit and stirring frequently. Boil rapidly 15 minutes. Stir in and dissolve sugar. Boil again very quickly for 15 minutes. Pot and cover at once.

Fruit	Season	Preparation	Water	Sugar	Method
Rhubarb	July	Wipe, trim, cut up	None. Use strained juice of 1 lemon to 3 lb.	14 oz per lb fruit	Cook slowly in pan with lemon juice, or 1 level teaspoonful citric acid to 3 lb fruit until pulped. Add sugar and dissolve, and 1 teaspoonful ground ginger. Boil very quickly ½ hour, stirring constantly. Pot and cover at once.
Greengage ripe fruit	August	Wash and drain	None	14 oz per lb fruit	Pull fruit in halves over pan to remove stones – then no juice will be wasted. Stir while slowly bringing to boil. Lift from stove while adding sugar; dissolve thoroughly. Bring again to boil. Boil briskly 15 minutes. Stir few minutes after removing pan from stove. Pot and seal immediately. Stones from fruit may be put into muslin, securely fastened, and cooked in preserve for flavour. If liked a few kernels, split in halves, may be added to jam.
Greengage unripe	August	Wash and drain	1 gill per lb	1 lb per lb fruit	Cook fruit in water until pulped, lift out stones and drain back all juice. Add sugar. Method as ripe greengages.
Blackberry early cultivated varieties	August	Use only sound fruit. Mix in few under-ripe berries. Rinse and drain.	¾ gill per lb	1 lb per lb fruit	Cook fruit and water together by simmering only. When pulped, press through sieve. Rub nut of butter over bottom of pan. Pour in juice, stir in and dissolve sugar. Boil rapidly 15 minutes, then test. Pot and cover at once.
Plum unripe	August	Stalk, wash or wipe	¾ gill per lb	1 lb per lb fruit	As for Greengage Jam.
Plum ripe	August September	Stalk, wash or wipe	None	1 lb per lb fruit	Cook fruit over low heat on stove, or in jar in oven. When soft,

Fruit	Season	Preparation	Water	Sugar	Method
Plum *contd.* ripe					remove stones, stir in sugar. When dissolved, boil rapidly. Test after 15 minutes. Pot and cover.
Apricot	August	Stalk, wash or wipe. Remove stones.	1 gill per lb	1 lb per lb fruit	As for ripe plums. Crack a few stones and cook some kernels with jam.
Apple & Blackberry	September	Peel and slice apples. Rinse blackberries in slightly salted water, drain.	Apples, 1 gill per lb. Blackberries, none.	1 lb per lb for each fruit	Boil apples with water until pulped. Cook blackberries over moderate heat until soft. Combine the two pulps. Stir in and dissolve sugar. Boil 20 minutes. Pot and cover.
Damson	September	Stalk and wash	1 gill per lb	1 lb per lb fruit	Simmer with water about 20 to 25 minutes until tender. Remove stones, add sugar and dissolve. Boil rapidly 10 to 15 minutes. Pot and cover.

CHAPTER THREE
Jams

Jams can be made from an enormous variety of fruit, and even from some vegetables such as marrows and carrots. Combinations of fruit are almost endless, and often glut fruit such as apples and rhubarb can be combined with small quantities of more special fruit such as raspberries to provide a larger amount of delicious jam than would be possible with the raspberries alone. Also included in this chapter are the 'marmalades' of fresh fruit, rich mixtures of fruit and sugar which are particularly suitable for filling tarts or providing an elegant finish for puddings.

Full details of the necessary equipment and ingredients for all types of jams will be found in Chapter One.

Fruit for jam should be well washed and drained, and all stems, leaves and bruised parts removed. Stoned fruit may be left whole, or the stones removed during cooking. The kernels of some of the stones can be included in apricot, cherry, plum and greengage jams, giving a slight almond flavour.

The fruit should then be cooked in the given amount of water until completely tender. Once this is done and the contents of the pan are considerably reduced, the pan should be removed from the heat, and the sugar stirred in until dissolved. The jam must then be boiled rapidly to setting point. A test should be made after 5 minutes; few jams need to boil longer than 20 minutes.

Setting is most easily tested by putting a little jam on to a cool plate. When the jam is cool, the surface should wrinkle when pushed with a finger. The jam should not boil while this test is being taken, or the setting point may be missed. Jam is also ready when a sugar thermometer gives a reading of 220°F, or when it flakes cleanly from a wooden spoon.

Jam should be skimmed at the end of boiling, rather than a number of times during the process. Fruit will rise in the jars if the jam does not cool for a minute or two before being potted. A waxed disc must be put on at once, and carefully pressed to exclude air bubbles. Finally the rims of the jars should be wiped and the jars covered. Circles of Cellophane should be damped on one side only and stretched tightly over hot or cold jars, making sure the underside is dry. Finally the jars should be labelled and stored in a cool dry place.

Apple Jam (1)

> 3 lb cooking apples
> 1 pint water
> 2 teaspoons citric acid
> 6 cloves
> Sugar

Do not peel or core the apples, cut them into slices. Put into the pan with water, acid and cloves and simmer to a pulp. Remove the cloves, and sieve apples. Weigh the pulp and allow 12 oz sugar to each lb pulp. Stir sugar until dissolved, then boil hard to setting point. Pour into hot jars.

Apple Jam (2)

> 3 lb cooking apples
> 2¼ lb sugar
> 3 lemons

Peel and core the fruit. Cut it into slices and put into an earthenware jar with the sugar and the grated rinds and juice of the lemons. Stand the jar in a large pan of water and simmer for about 30 minutes until cooked. Skim and pour into hot jars. This jam is also delicious if flavoured with a handful of peach leaves tied into a muslin bag and removed before potting.

Apple & Apricot Jam

> 2 lb cooking apples
> 2 lb fresh apricots
> 1 pint water
> 4 lb sugar

Peel and core the apples and cut them in pieces. Cut the apricots in half and remove the stones. Simmer the fruit in the water until soft. Stir in the sugar until dissolved, then boil hard to setting point. Pour into hot jars.

Apple & Ginger Jam

> 3 lb cooking apples
> 3 lb sugar
> 1 pint water
> 4 oz crystallised ginger
> 1 teaspoon ground ginger
> 2 lemons

Peel and core the apples and cut them into pieces· Put the peel and cores into a muslin bag and suspend them in the pan. Put apples and water into the pan with the ground ginger and the grated rind and juice of the lemons. Simmer until the fruit is tender. Remove the bag of peel and squeeze out the juice. Stir in the sugar and chopped ginger until the sugar has dissolved, then boil hard to setting point. Pour into hot jars.

Apple & Green Tomato Jam

> 2 lb cooking apples
> 3 lb green tomatoes
> 1 pint water
> 1½ teaspoons ground ginger
> ½ teaspoon ground cloves
> 3½ lb sugar

Peel, core and slice the apples thinly. Slice the tomatoes thinly, and simmer in the water for 5 minutes. Add apples and spices and simmer until soft. Stir in the sugar until dissolved, then boil hard to setting point. Pour into hot jars.

Apple & Orange Jam

$2\frac{1}{2}$ lb cooking apples
3 oranges
$\frac{1}{2}$ pint water
$2\frac{1}{4}$ lb sugar

Peel, core and slice the apples and put into the water with the grated orange rind. Simmer until soft and then add the cut-up oranges. Simmer 10 minutes, then stir in the sugar until dissolved. Boil hard to setting point, and pour into hot jars.

Apple, Pear & Plum Jam

$1\frac{1}{2}$ lb cooking apples
$1\frac{1}{2}$ lb ripe pears
$1\frac{1}{2}$ lb plums
$3\frac{3}{4}$ lb sugar
$\frac{1}{2}$ oz root ginger

Peel and core the apples and pears. Skin and stone the plums. Put the fruit into a pan, and add the bruised root ginger tied into a muslin bag. Simmer until the fruit is soft but not broken, adding a little water if necessary to prevent burning. Stir in the sugar until dissolved, then boil hard to setting point. Remove the ginger, and pour into hot jars. This is sometimes known as Mock Apricot Jam.

Apple & Pineapple Jam

1¼ lb cooking apples
1 lb prepared fresh pineapple
½ pint water
2 lb sugar

Peel and core the apples and cut into pieces. Cut the pineapple into small pieces. Simmer together in the water until soft. Stir in the sugar until dissolved, then boil hard to setting point. Pour into hot jars.

Apricot Jam (Fresh Fruit)

6 lb fresh apricots
¾ pint water
Juice of 1 lemon
6 lb sugar

Cut the apricots in half and remove the stones. Take the kernels from some of the stones, blanch them in boiling water, and put halved kernels with the fruit. Put fruit, water and kernels into a pan and simmer until the fruit is very soft. Stir in the sugar until dissolved, then boil hard to setting point. Pour into hot jars.

Banana Jam

2 lb bananas (weighed after peeling)
1½ pint orange juice
Juice of 2 lemons
1¼ lb sugar

Cut bananas in slices and add fruit juices. Put into an earthenware jar and stand the jar in a pan of water. Bring mixture to the boil. Stir in sugar until dissolved, then boil about 10 minutes until thick and red. Skim and stir all the time. Pour into hot jars.

Blackberry Jam

6 lb blackberries
¼ pint water
4 teaspoons lemon juice
6 lb sugar

Put the blackberries into a pan with the water and lemon juice. Simmer until the fruit is very soft. Stir in the sugar until dissolved, then boil hard to setting point. Pour into hot jars.

Blackberry & Apple Jam

4 lb blackberries
2 lb cooking apples
½ pint water
6 lb sugar

Put the blackberries in a pan with half the water and simmer until tender. Peel, core and slice the apples, and cook in the remaining water until tender. Combine the two fruits. Stir in the sugar until dissolved, then boil hard to setting point. Pour into hot jars. Two tablespoons rum may be stirred in before potting.

Blackberry & Elderberry Jam

2 lb blackberries
2 lb elderberries
3 lb sugar

Strip the elderberries from their stalks, and put with the blackberries into a pan. Simmer for 20 minutes, crushing the berries with a wooden spoon. Stir in the sugar until dissolved, then boil hard to setting point. Pour into hot jars.

Blackberry & Marrow Jam

2 lb blackberries
4 lb prepared marrow
Grated rind of 1 lemon
Juice of 2 lemons
1 pint water
3½ lb sugar

Put the blackberries and the marrow cut into cubes into a pan with the lemon rind and juice and the water. Simmer until soft, and then put through a sieve. Stir in the sugar until dissolved, then boil hard to setting point. Pour into hot jars.

Blackberry & Pear Jam

4 lb ripe pears
4 lb blackberries
Juice of 1 lemon
Sugar

Peel and core the pears, and cut into small pieces. Cover 3 lb blackberries with water and simmer to a pulp, then strain through a jelly bag. Measure the blackberry juice and allow 12 oz sugar to each pint of juice. Put blackberry juice, pears, remaining blackberries and lemon juice into a pan and bring to the boil. Simmer for 30 minutes. Stir in the sugar until dissolved, then boil hard to setting point. Pour into hot jars.

Blackberry & Pineapple Jam

1 lb blackberries
1 lb cooking apples
1 medium fresh pineapple
Juice of 3 lemons
3 lb sugar

Peel, core and slice the apples. Cut up the pineapple to make 1 lb cubes. Put apples and pineapple in a pan with just enough water to prevent burning and simmer for 15 minutes. Add the blackberries and simmer for 10 minutes. Stir in lemon juice and sugar until the sugar has dissolved, then boil hard to setting point. Pour into hot jars.

Blackberry & Rhubarb Jam

4 lb blackberries
2 lb rhubarb
¾ pint water
Sugar

Simmer blackberries in water until tender and put through a sieve. Cut up rhubarb and put into blackberry pulp. Simmer until soft. Weigh the fruit and add 1 lb sugar to each lb pulp. Stir in sugar until dissolved, then boil hard to setting point. Pour into hot jars.

Blackcurrant Jam

4 lb blackcurrants
6 lb sugar
3 pints water

Remove the stems and wash the fruit. Put blackcurrants into a pan with the water and simmer gently until the fruit is very tender. Stir often to prevent burning. Stir in sugar until dissolved and then boil hard to setting point. Pour into hot jars.

Blackcurrant & Cherry Jam

2 lb blackcurrants
2 lb black cherries
1 pint water
3 lb sugar

Simmer the blackcurrants in the water for 1 hour, and put through a jelly bag. Simmer stoned cherries in the blackcurrant juice for 20 minutes. Stir in the sugar until dissolved, then boil hard to setting point. Pour into hot jars.

Carrot Jam

> 1 lb young carrots
> 1 lb sugar
> 2 lemons
> 6 blanched almonds
> 2 tablespoons brandy

Scrape the carrots and cut into pieces. Simmer in just enough water to cover until soft. Drain well and put through a sieve. Mix with sugar, and the grated rind and juice of the lemons. Stir well to dissolve sugar, then boil for 5 minutes, stirring well. Cool and stir in the almonds and brandy. Pour into jars. The jam will not keep without the brandy.

Cherry Jam

> 4 lb black cherries
> $\frac{1}{4}$ oz citric or tartaric acid
> $3\frac{1}{2}$ lb sugar

Remove the stones from the cherries. Crack about 24 stones and remove the kernels. Put the cherries, kernels and acid into a pan and simmer until very soft, stirring often. Stir in the sugar until dissolved, and then boil hard to setting point. Pour into hot jars. Cherry jam only sets lightly.

Cherry & Gooseberry Jam

3 lb Morello cherries
1½ lb red gooseberries
¼ oz tartaric acid
4 lb sugar

Stone the cherries, and top and tail the gooseberries. Put into a pan and heat until the juice flows. Add the acid and simmer until the fruit is soft. Stir in the sugar until dissolved, then boil hard to setting point. Pour into hot jars.

Cherry & Orange Jam

4 lb black cherries
4 thin-skinned oranges
1 gill lemon juice
2 cinnamon sticks
6 cloves
3½ lb granulated sugar

Stone the cherries, and if liked crack a few of the stones and remove the kernels, blanching them before use. Cut the oranges in very thin slices. Just cover with water, and add the cinnamon and cloves tied into a muslin bag. Simmer until the oranges are tender, and take out spice bag. Add the cherries, lemon juice, kernels and sugar. Stir until the sugar has dissolved, then boil hard to setting point. Pour into hot jars.

Cranberry Jam

4 lb cranberries
¾ pint water
4 lb sugar

Simmer the cranberries in the water until the skins burst and are soft. Stir in the sugar until dissolved, then boil hard to setting point. Pour into hot jars.

Cranberry & Apple Jam

$1\frac{1}{2}$ lb cranberries
$1\frac{1}{2}$ lb cooking apples
$\frac{1}{2}$ pint water
3 lb sugar

Put the cranberries into a pan with the peeled, cored and sliced apples and the water. Simmer until fruit is soft. Stir in the sugar until dissolved, then boil hard to setting point. Pour into hot jars.

Cranberry & Pumpkin Jam

8 oz cranberries
$3\frac{1}{2}$ lb prepared pumpkin
1 pint water
1 teaspoon tartaric acid
4 lb sugar

Put the cranberries with the diced pumpkin flesh, water and acid into a pan and simmer for about 1 hour until tender. Stir in the sugar until dissolved, then boil hard to setting point.

Damson Jam

$2\frac{1}{2}$ lb damsons
$\frac{3}{4}$ pint water
3 lb sugar

Simmer the damsons in the water until soft. Stir in the sugar until dissolved, then boil hard to setting point. Remove the stones as they rise in the pan. Pour into hot jars.

Damson & Marrow Jam

> 3 lb damsons
> 3 lb prepared marrow
> 1 pint water
> Sugar

Simmer the damsons in half the water until tender, and then put through a sieve. Cut the marrow flesh into small pieces and cook in the remaining water until soft. Mix the damson and marrow pulps and weigh the fruit. Allow 1 lb sugar to each lb of fruit pulp. Stir in the sugar until dissolved, then boil hard to setting point. Pour into hot jars.

Damson & Pear Jam

> 2 lb damsons
> 2 lb pears
> ½ pint water
> 4 lb sugar

Cut up the peeled and cored pears. Put pears and damsons with water in a pan and simmer until tender, removing the damson stones as they rise to the surface. Stir in the sugar until dissolved, then boil hard to setting point. Pour into hot jars.

Gooseberry Jam

> 6 lb gooseberries
> 2 pints water
> 6 lb sugar

Use slightly under-ripe gooseberries. Top and tail them, and put into a pan with the water. Simmer for 30 minutes, mashing the fruit, and stirring well. Stir in the sugar until dissolved, then boil hard to setting point. Pour into hot jars. Gooseberry jam will remain green if made from a variety which remains green even when ripe; prolonged boiling after the sugar is added will darken the colour. Jam made from fully-ripe or dessert gooseberries will yield a pink jam with a light set. A few elderflower heads tied in muslin and suspended in the jam will give a delicious muscat flavour.

Ettrick Jam

> 4 lb green gooseberries
> 4 lb sugar
> 1 lemon

Top and tail the gooseberries and simmer with a little water until soft. Stir in the sugar until dissolved, and add the grated rind and juice of the lemon. Boil hard for exactly 10 minutes, then pour into hot jars.

Greengage Jam

> 6 lb greengages
> 1 pint water
> 6 lb sugar

Cut the greengages in half and remove the stones. Take the kernels from some of the stones, blanch them in boiling water, and put halved kernels with the fruit. Put fruit, water and kernels into a pan and simmer until the fruit is very soft. Stir in the sugar until dissolved, then boil hard to setting point. Pour into hot jars.

Japonica Jam

> 4 lb japonica fruit
> 6 pints water
> 2 teaspoons ground cloves
> Sugar

The japonica fruit is a type of quince, and good for jam-making. Slice the fruit and simmer in the water until tender. Put through a sieve and weigh the pulp. Add an equal weight of sugar, and stir until dissolved. Bring to the boil and add ground cloves. Boil hard to setting point, and pour into hot jars.

Loganberry Jam

3 lb loganberries
3 lb sugar

Simmer the loganberries for 20 minutes, stirring occasionally. Warm the sugar and stir into the berries until dissolved. Boil hard for about 10 minutes to setting point. Pour into hot jars.

Marrow Jam

6 lb prepared marrow
4 lemons
3 oz root ginger
6 lb sugar

Cut the peeled marrow into cubes and steam until just tender. Put into a bowl with the grated rind and juice of the lemons, the bruised root ginger tied in a muslin bag, and the sugar. Leave for 24 hours. Put into a pan and heat carefully until the sugar is dissolved. Cook until the marrow is transparent and the syrup is thick. Pour into hot jars.

Peach Jam

2 lb peaches
1½ lb sugar
Juice of 1 lemon
2 teaspoons rose-water
2 teaspoons orange flower water

35

Dip the peaches into boiling water, put into cold water, and remove their skins. Cut the peaches in quarters and take out their stones and put into a pan with the lemon juice. Simmer very gently until peaches soften, adding a little water if necessary to prevent burning. Stir in the sugar until dissolved, then boil hard to setting point. Stir in rose-water and orange flower water, simmer for 1 minute, and pour into hot jars.

Pear Jam

>   4 lb cooking pears
>   4 lb granulated sugar
>   1 dessertspoon ground ginger
>   2 lemons

Peel and core the pears. Chop or mince the flesh, and put into a bowl with the sugar. Leave overnight. Put the fruit and sugar into a pan with the ginger, grated rind and juice of the lemons. Simmer until the fruit is tender, then boil hard to setting point. Pour into hot jars.

Pear & Pineapple Jam

>   3 lb eating pears
>   1 small fresh pineapple
>   5 lemons
>   4 lb sugar
>   Miniature bottle of kirsch

Peel and core the pears and cut into small pieces. Peel the pineapple and chop it finely. Put pears, pineapple and grated rind and juice of the lemons into a pan and simmer for 10 minutes. Stir in the sugar until dissolved, then boil hard to setting point. Stir in kirsch and reheat without boiling. Pour into hot jars.

Pineapple Jam (Fresh Fruit)

3 lb pineapple
¾ pint water
Juice of 1 lemon
2½ lb sugar

Weigh the pineapple after the fruit has been peeled and trimmed. Shred the pineapple, discarding the central core. Add to water and lemon juice and simmer until the pineapple is tender and the water has evaporated. Stir in the sugar until dissolved, then boil hard to setting point. Pour into hot jars.

Plum Jam

6 lb plums
1 pint water
6 lb sugar

Cut the plums in half and remove the stones. Take the kernels from some of the stones, blanch them in boiling water, and put halved kernels with the fruit. Put fruit, water and kernels into a pan and simmer until the fruit is very soft. Stir in the sugar until dissolved, then boil hard to setting point. Pour into hot jars.

Plum & Apple Jam

2 lb plums
2 lb cooking apples
1½ pints water
3 lb sugar

Cut the plums in half and remove the stones. Peel and core the apples, and cut in slices. Put the plums and apples into a pan with the water and simmer until soft. Stir in the sugar until dissolved, then boil hard to setting point. Pour into hot jars.

Plum & Marrow Jam

                1 lb plums
                2 lb prepared marrow
                2 lb sugar

Cut the plums in half and remove the stones. Cut the marrow flesh into cubes, sprinkle it with sugar and leave to stand for 1 hour. Put plums, marrow and remaining sugar into a pan and simmer until the fruit is tender. Boil hard to setting point and pour into hot jars.

Raspberry Jam

                4 lb raspberries
                4 lb sugar

Wash the fruit and simmer in its own juice for 20 minutes. Stir in the sugar until dissolved, then boil hard to setting point. Pour into hot jars.

Raspberry & Peach Jam

                2 lb raspberries
                2 lb peaches
                1 gill water
                3 lb sugar

Peel and stone the peaches and cut into pieces. Crack some of the stones, and put the kernels with the peaches into the water. Simmer until tender. Stir in the raspberries and sugar, and when the sugar has dissolved, boil hard to setting point. Pour into hot jars.

Raspberry & Redcurrant Jam

                $1\frac{1}{2}$ lb raspberries
                $1\frac{1}{2}$ lb redcurrants
                1 pint water
                3 lb sugar

Wash the raspberries, and wash and string the red-currants. Put into the pan with the water and simmer for 20 minutes. Stir in the sugar until dissolved, then boil hard to setting point. Pour into hot jars.

Raspberry & Rhubarb Jam

> 3 lb raspberries
> 3 lb rhubarb
> ½ pint water
> 6 lb sugar

Cut the rhubarb into pieces and simmer in the water until soft. Add the raspberries and cook until soft. Stir in the sugar until dissolved, then boil hard to setting point. Pour into hot jars.

Rhubarb & Fig Jam

> 2 lb rhubarb
> 8 oz dried figs
> 2 lb sugar
> Juice of 1 lemon

Cut the rhubarb into pieces and the figs into small chunks. Mix with sugar and lemon juice and leave to stand for 24 hours. Bring to the boil, and boil rapidly to setting point. Leave to cool for 15 minutes, stir well, and pour into jars.

Rhubarb & Orange Jam

> 2 lb rhubarb
> 6 oranges
> Sugar

Cut the rhubarb into neat pieces. Grate the orange rinds. Remove white pith and cut up the orange flesh. Weigh the rhubarb and oranges together and allow

1 lb sugar, to each lb mixed fruit. Soak the orange pips in hot water. Simmer the rhubarb, orange flesh and rind together until reduced to half. Stir in the sugar until dissolved, together with the water strained from the pips. Boil hard to setting point, and pour into hot jars.

Strawberry Jam (1)

    4 lb strawberries
    1 teaspoon citric or tartaric acid
    3½ lb sugar

Put the strawberries in a pan with the acid and simmer for 30 minutes until the fruit is soft. Stir in the sugar until dissolved, then boil hard to setting point. Cool for 15 minutes, stir well, and pour into hot jars.

Strawberry Jam (2)

    3½ lb strawberries
    3 tablespoons lemon juice
    3 lb sugar

Put the strawberries in a pan with the lemon juice and simmer for 30 minutes until the fruit is soft. Stir in the sugar until dissolved, then boil hard to setting point. Cool for 15 minutes, stir well, and pour into hot jars.

Strawberry Jam (3)

    4 lb strawberries
    4 lb sugar

Put the strawberries into a bowl with the sugar in layers and leave overnight. Put into a pan and bring to the boil. Boil for 5 minutes and return to the bowl. Leave overnight, then boil hard to setting point. Cool for 15 minutes, stir well, and pour into hot jars.

Green Tomato Jam

>   2 lb green tomatoes
>   Rind of 1 sweet orange
>   1½ lb sugar

Shred the orange rind very finely and simmer in as little water as possible until tender. Cut up the tomatoes and simmer with the orange rind until tender. Stir in the sugar until dissolved, then boil hard to setting point. Pour into hot jars.

Red Tomato Jam

>   6 lb ripe tomatoes
>   10 tablespoons lemon juice
>   2 teaspoons citric or tartaric acid
>   6 lb sugar

Skin the tomatoes. Cut them into pieces and put into a pan with the lemon juice and acid. Simmer to a pulp. Stir in the sugar until dissolved, then boil hard to setting point. Pour into hot jars.

Four Fruit Jam

>   8 oz blackcurrants
>   8 oz redcurrants
>   8 oz raspberries
>   8 oz strawberries
>   2 lb sugar

Put the blackcurrants in a pan with very little water and simmer until tender. Add other fruit and simmer for 10 minutes. Stir in the sugar until dissolved, then boil hard to setting point. Pour into hot jars.

Apricot Marmalade (Fresh Fruit)

>   3½ lb ripe apricots
>   2¼ lb sugar

Cut the fruit in half and put into an earthenware jar in a pan of water. Simmer for 30 minutes and put through a sieve. Add the kernels from some of the stones and reheat. Stir in the sugar and boil hard, stirring all the time, until the bottom of the pan can be seen. Pour into hot jars.

Greengage Marmalade

Ripe greengages
Sugar

Stone the greengages and weigh them. Boil fast without any water for 45 minutes. Stir in 12 oz sugar to each lb fruit until dissolved. Boil hard for 5 minutes, stirring all the time, and pour into hot jars.

Peach & Pineapple Marmalade

7 lb peaches
1 large pineapple
3 lemons
6 lb sugar

Peel and stone the peaches, and remove the kernels from about half the stones. Peel and slice the pineapple, and cut into small pieces. Put the fruit into a pan with very little water, and simmer for 30 minutes. Stir in the sugar, the juice of the lemons and the kernels, and boil for 20 minutes. Pour into hot jars.

Pear Marmalade

6 lb pears
1 pint sweet cider
4 lb sugar
Juice of 1 lemon
Pink colouring

Do not peel or core the pears, but cut into small pieces. Heat the cider and then add the pears and simmer gently until tender. Put through a sieve. Return to the pan with the sugar and lemon and stir until the sugar is dissolved. Boil moderately fast, stirring constantly to setting point. Tint lightly with pink colouring and pour into hot jars.

Pineapple Marmalade

Pineapples
Sugar

Peel the pineapples, removing any dark spots, and slice the fruit very thinly, removing the core. Pulp the fruit in a mortar or a blender. Weigh the pulp, and then bring it to the boil. Stir in 14 oz sugar for each lb fruit until dissolved. Boil hard for 15 minutes and pour into hot jars. The marmalade will be thick and transparent.

Strawberry & Pineapple Marmalade

½ pint crushed strawberries
½ pint crushed pineapple
½ pint orange juice
Juice of 4 lemons
3½ lb sugar

Simmer the strawberries and pineapple until tender. Stir in the strained orange juice, the sugar and the strained lemon juice. Stir until sugar has dissolved, then boil hard to setting point. Pour into hot jars.

CHAPTER FOUR
Jellies

No special equipment is needed for jelly-making, except a jelly bag or cloth. Jellies are very simple to make and most rewarding, but it is important to pay attention to careful measurements and cooking details. The perfect jelly should be sparkling and clear with a bright colour and fresh fruit flavour. It should be sufficiently stiff to retain its shape when spooned from the jar.

All fruits should be washed before cooking starts. Hard fruits (such as apples and quinces) should be sliced without peeling and coring. Stone fruits should be washed and cut in half. Soft fruits may usually be left on their stems. Fruit should be lightly crushed in the cooking pan with a wooden spoon to start the juices flowing.

Fruit should be ripe but not over-ripe. If possible, a small proportion of under-ripe fruit should be included to give a good set (about $\frac{1}{4}$ lb under-ripe fruit to $\frac{3}{4}$ lb ripe fruit). Apples, redcurrants and gooseberries are rich in pectin and have a good setting quality. They can usefully be combined with other fruits which will not set so well on their own.

Put the fruit into a preserving pan with water. Some berries and currants require no water, but blackcurrants and hard fruits need water to help soften their skins. Generally hard fruit should be covered with water. Fruit which is to simmer in its own juice is better cooked in a covered jar in the oven or standing in a pan of hot water. Fruit should be simmered very slowly to extract all pectin and acid, and the fruit must be very tender before straining. To save the long cooking time necessary ($\frac{3}{4}$ to 1 hour) fruit can be prepared for jelly in a pressure cooker, with only half the usual amount of water. Apples require 7 minutes at 10 lb pressure; damsons 5 minutes; blackcurrants 4 minutes and gooseberries 3 minutes. The fruit is then strained and finished in the usual way.

Fruit pulp must be strained through a jelly bag or piece of muslin which has been scalded. This may be suspended from a hook or from the four legs of an up-turned chair. Let the juice drip slowly into a bowl, and do not squeeze, stir or shake the bag, or the jelly will be cloudy. The dripping process may take an hour, or overnight. The liquid should then be measured and sugar weighed out accordingly. Usually 1 lb sugar is allowed to each pint of juice for fruit rich in pectin and acid, but 12 oz sugar can be used for fruit of a poorer setting quality.

Some people like to warm the sugar before adding it to the juice. This is not really necessary, but will speed up the dissolving process. The juice should be slowly heated and the sugar stirred in until it has dissolved. The jelly should then be boiled rapidly to setting point. Apple and gooseberry jellies have a better colour if cold sugar is added to cold juice.

Jellies should be boiled to 220°F, when the jelly will partly set on the spoon, and drops will run together to form flakes which drop cleanly from the spoon. Jelly should be skimmed carefully with a metal spoon dipped in boiling water. It should be poured into 1 lb jars, or smaller ones, and the jars tilted as the jelly is poured in down the sides to avoid air bubbles. Cover the jelly with waxed circles at once, and put on the top cover either at once or when the jelly is completely cold. Jelly should not be moved until it has set, and should be stored in a cool dry place.

Jellies can be used for spreads, but are also useful for glazing fruit, cakes and flans. Some jellies are excellent eaten with meat, fish, poultry or game. When the juice has been extracted, the pulp of such fruit as damsons can be sieved and then used for fruit cheeses (see Chapter Eight BUTTERS AND CHEESES)

Apple Jelly

6 lb cooking apples
Juice of 2 lemons
Sugar

47

Windfall apples may be used, but bruised and damaged portions should be removed before weighing. Do not peel or core the apples. Cut them into pieces and put into a pan with the lemon juice and enough water to cover. Simmer until the apples are soft and the liquid reduced by about one-third. Strain through a jelly bag. Measure the liquid and allow 1 lb sugar to a pint of liquid. Bring to the boil, stirring until the sugar has dissolved. Boil hard to setting point. Skim, pour into hot jars, and cover.

A few blackberries, cranberries, currants or raspberries may be added to give the apple jelly a good colour. Apple jelly is used as a basis for many other jellies, since it has a high pectin content and sets well; it is particularly good used with fresh herbs to make jellies to eat with meat or poultry. Plain apple jelly is delicious when one or two rose-geranium leaves are simmered with the apple pulp.

Blackberry & Apple Jelly

> 4 lb blackberries
> 2 lb cooking apples
> 2 pints water
> Sugar

Put the blackberries into a pan with the apples which have been cut up but not peeled or cored. Simmer with the water for 1 hour until the fruit is soft. Strain through a jelly bag and measure the juice. Allow 1 lb sugar to each pint of juice. Heat the juice gently, stirring in the sugar until dissolved. Boil hard to setting point, and pour into hot jars.

Blackberry & Sloe Jelly

> 4 lb blackberries
> 1 lb sloes
> Sugar

48

Put the blackberries into a pan with the sloes which have been pricked. Cover with water and simmer until tender. Strain through a jelly bag and measure the juice. Allow 1 lb sugar to each pint of juice. Heat the juice gently, stirring in the sugar until dissolved. Boil hard to setting point and pour into hot jars.

Blackcurrant Jelly

4 lb blackcurrants
3 pints water
Sugar

Simmer blackcurrants in water for 1 hour until soft. Strain through a jelly bag and measure the juice. Allow 1 lb sugar to each pint of juice. Heat the juice gently, stirring in the sugar until dissolved. Boil hard to setting point and pour into hot jars.

Blackcurrant & Apple Jelly

4 lb blackcurrants
2 lb cooking apples
4 pints water
Sugar

Put the blackcurrants into a pan with the apples cut into slices but not peeled and cored. Simmer with water for 1 hour until the fruit is very soft. Strain through a jelly bag and measure the juice. Allow 1 lb sugar to each pint of juice. Heat the juice gently, stirring in the sugar until dissolved. Boil hard to setting point and pour into hot jars.

Blackcurrant & Redcurrant Jelly

1 lb blackcurrants
1 lb redcurrants
1 pint water
Sugar

Simmer the currants in water until soft. Strain through a jelly bag and measure the juice. Allow 1 lb sugar to each pint of juice. Heat the juice gently, stirring in the sugar until dissolved. Boil hard to setting point and pour into hot jars.

Bramble (Blackberry) Jelly

4 lb blackberries
Juice of 2 lemons
½ pint water
Sugar

It is better to use slightly under-ripe blackberries. Put them into a pan with the lemon juice and water and simmer for 1 hour until the fruit is soft. Strain through a jelly bag and measure the juice. Allow 1 lb sugar to each pint of juice. Heat the juice gently, stirring in the sugar until dissolved. Boil hard to setting point and pour into hot jars. The jelly may be spiced with the addition of ¼ teaspoon each of ground mace, nutmeg and cinnamon.

Blueberry Jelly

3 lb blueberries
3 lb cooking apples
Juice of 2 lemons
Sugar

Blueberries are also known as bilberries, whinberries, huckleberries and whortleberries. Remove the stalks from the fruit, and slice the apples without peeling or coring. Cover the fruit with water and simmer until tender, crushing the berries well. Strain through a jelly bag and measure the juice. Allow 1 lb sugar to each pint of juice. Stir in the lemon juice and sugar until the sugar has dissolved. Boil hard to setting point. Pour into hot jars and cover.

Crabapple Jelly

> 4 lb crabapples
> 2 pints water
> 6 cloves
> Sugar

Do not peel or core the fruit. Cut into quarters and put into a pan with the water and the cloves. Bring to the boil, and then simmer until the apples are very soft. Add a little more water if the fruit is boiling dry. Strain through a jelly bag and measure the juice. Allow 1 lb sugar to each pint of juice. Heat the juice gently and stir in the sugar until dissolved. Boil hard to setting point and pour into hot jars.

Crabapple & Rowanberry Jelly

> 2 lb rowanberries
> 1 lb crabapples
> Sugar

The rowanberries should be very ripe. Remove stalks from the berries and put into the pan with the crabapples which have been cut up but not peeled and cored. Add just enough water to cover and simmer until the fruit is soft. Strain through a jelly bag and measure the juice. Allow 1 lb sugar to each pint of juice. Heat the juice gently, stirring in the sugar until dissolved. Boil hard to setting point, and pour into hot jars. This is very good as a spread, or eaten with roast lamb or game.

Cranberry Jelly

> 2 lb cranberries
> 1 pint water
> Sugar

Cook the cranberries with the water very gently until the fruit is tender. Strain through a jelly bag and measure the juice. Allow 1 lb sugar to each pint of juice. Heat the juice gently, stirring in the sugar until dissolved. Boil hard to setting point and pour into hot jars. This can be used as a spread, or eaten with turkey, chicken or game.

Cranberry & Apple Jelly

> 2 lb cranberries
> 4 sweet oranges
> 3 lb cooking apples
> 3¼ pints water
> Sugar

Cut the oranges and apples into pieces without peeling and coring or removing pith. Add the cranberries and simmer in the water for 1½ hours until the fruit and peel are tender. Strain through a jelly bag and measure the juice. Allow 1 lb sugar to each pint of juice. Heat the juice gently, stirring in the sugar until dissolved. Boil hard to setting point and pour into hot jars. This may be used as a spread or with chicken, turkey or game.

Cranberry & Grape Jelly

> 1 lb cranberries
> 1 lb white grapes
> ¼ pint water
> Lemon juice
> Sugar

Simmer the cranberries and grapes in the water until soft. Strain through a jelly bag and measure the liquid.

Allow 1 lb sugar and the juice of 1 lemon to each pint of liquid. Stir until the sugar has dissolved. Boil hard to setting point, and pour into hot jars.

Damson Jelly

6 lb damsons
3 pints water
Sugar

Simmer damsons in water for 1 hour until soft. Strain through a jelly bag and measure the juice. Allow 1 lb sugar to each pint of juice. Heat the juice gently, stirring in the sugar until dissolved. Boil hard to setting point and pour into hot jars.

Elderberry & Apple Jelly

2 lb elderberries
2 lb cooking or crab apples
2 pints water
Sugar

Pick elderberries from their stalks and mix with apples cut in pieces but not peeled and cored. Cover with water and simmer for 1 hour until the fruit is soft. Strain through a jelly bag and measure the juice. Allow 1 lb sugar to each pint of juice. Heat the juice gently, stirring in the sugar until dissolved. Boil hard to setting point and pour into hot jars.

Elderberry & Blackberry Jelly

2 lb elderberries
2 lb blackberries
2 pints water
Sugar

Pick elderberries from their stalks and mix with the blackberries. Cover with water and simmer for 1 hour until the fruit is soft. Strain through a jelly bag and measure the juice. Allow 1 lb sugar to each pint of juice. Heat the juice gently, stirring in the sugar until dissolved. Boil hard to setting point and pour into hot jars.

Elderberry Four Fruit Jelly

3½ lb elderberries
1 lb apples
1 lb damsons
1 lb blackberries
1 teaspoon ground cloves
1 teaspoon ground allspice
½ teaspoon ground ginger
Pinch of cinnamon
2 pints water
2 lb sugar

Pick elderberries from their stalks. Mix with apples cut in pieces but not peeled or cored, damsons and blackberries. Add water and spices and simmer for 1 hour until the fruit is soft. Strain through a jelly bag and measure the juice. Allow 1 lb sugar to each pint of juice. Heat the juice gently, stirring in the sugar until dissolved. Boil hard to setting point and pour into hot jars.

Gooseberry Jelly

4 lb gooseberries
Sugar

Do not top and tail the gooseberries but put them into a pan with just enough water to cover. Simmer for 1 hour until the fruit is very soft. Strain through a jelly bag and measure the juice. Allow 1 lb sugar to each pint of juice. Heat the juice gently, stirring in the sugar until dissolved. Boil hard to setting point and pour into hot jars. This jelly is particularly delicious if a bunch of elderflower heads is tied into muslin and trailed in the juice while it is being cooked with the sugar. The flavour resembles that of muscat grapes.

Gooseberry & Redcurrant Jelly

2 lb gooseberries
1 lb redcurrants
1 pint water
Sugar

Top and tail the gooseberries. Put with the redcurrants into the water, and simmer until the fruit is very soft. Strain through a jelly bag and measure the juice. Allow 1 lb sugar to each pint of juice. Heat the juice gently, stirring in the sugar until dissolved. Boil hard to setting point, and pour into hot jars.

Black Grape Jelly

Black grapes
Sugar

Use very good black grapes. Remove from stalks and stir very gently over a low heat until they burst. Strain through a jelly bag and measure the liquid. Boil for 20 minutes. Stir in 14 oz sugar to each pint of liquid and boil hard to setting point. Pour into hot jars.

Green Grape Jelly

Unripe grape thinnings
Sugar

Use grapes which are about the size of peas, and which have been thinned from bunches. Cover with water and simmer until soft. Strain through a jelly bag and measure the juice. Allow 1 lb sugar to each pint of juice. Heat the juice gently, stirring in the sugar until dissolved. Boil hard to setting point and pour into hot jars.

Hawthorn Jelly

2 lb ripe haws
1 pint water
Sugar

Remove stalks from the haws and put them into a pan with the water. Simmer until soft and then mash the fruit. Strain through a jelly bag and measure the juice. Allow 1 lb sugar to each pint of juice. Heat the juice gently, stirring in the sugar until dissolved. Boil hard to setting point and pour into hot jars.

Japonica Jelly

3 lb japonica fruit
4 tablespoons lemon juice
6 pints water
Sugar

The fruit of the japonica is a type of quince and makes very good jelly. Do not peel or core the fruit, but cut them into pieces. Add lemon juice and water and simmer for 1 hour until soft. Strain through a jelly bag and measure the juice. Allow 1 lb sugar to each pint of juice. Heat the juice gently, stirring in the sugar until dissolved. Boil hard to setting point and pour into hot jars.

Lemon Jelly (1)

4 lemons
1 lb sugar

Grate the rind of the lemons and squeeze out the juice. Put the rind, juice and sugar into the top of a double saucepan and cook over hot water. Cook until the mixture thickens and the jelly sheets from a spoon. Pour into hot jars, and cover.

Lemon Jelly (2)

6 lemons
3 pints water
Sugar

Slice the lemons thinly and put into a pan with the water. Tie the pips into a muslin bag and suspend in the saucepan. Bring to the boil and simmer for $1\frac{1}{2}$ hours. Strain through a jelly bag and measure the liquid. Allow 1 lb sugar to each pint of liquid. Heat the lemon juice to boiling point, stir in the sugar until dissolved. Boil hard to setting point. Skim, pour into hot jars, and cover.

Lemon Jelly (3)

1 pint lemon juice
$\frac{1}{2}$ pint water
Juice of 2 oranges
$1\frac{3}{4}$ lb sugar

Strain the lemon and orange juice and mix with the water. Boil for 10 minutes. Stir in the sugar until dissolved. Boil hard to setting point. Skim, pour into hot jars, and cover.

Loganberry Jelly

4 lb loganberries
$\frac{1}{2}$ pint water
Sugar

Use just ripe loganberries. Put into a pan with the water and simmer for 1 hour until soft. Strain through a jelly bag and measure the juice. Allow 1 lb sugar to each pint of juice. Heat the juice gently, stirring in the sugar until dissolved. Boil hard to setting point and pour into hot jars.

Mint Jelly (with Apples)

> Cooking apples
> White vinegar
> Sugar
> Fresh mint
> Green colouring

Cut up the apples without peeling or coring. Using $\frac{1}{4}$ pint vinegar to 1 pint water, just cover the apples. Add a good bunch of mint, and simmer until the fruit is soft and pulpy. Strain through a jelly bag, and measure liquid. Allow 1 lb sugar to each pint of liquid. Stir sugar until dissolved, then boil hard to setting point. Just before cooking is complete, add some finely chopped fresh mint and a few drops of green vegetable colouring. Skim well, cool slightly and stir well. Pour into small hot jars. Eat with roast lamb.

Sage, Parsley and Thyme Jellies may be made in the same way and are good with duck, pork and ham.

Bayleaf Jelly can be made in the same way, but without vinegar. No bay leaves should be added when the liquid is cooked with the sugar. This is good with fish and with chicken.

Mint Jelly (with Gooseberries or Redcurrants)

> 4 lb gooseberries or redcurrants
> Sugar
> Fresh mint

Cook the gooseberries or redcurrants with just enough water to cover. Strain through a jelly bag and measure the liquid. Allow 1 lb sugar to each pint of juice. Bring to the boil, stirring until the sugar has dissolved. Tie up a bunch of fresh mint, and hang this in the pan. Boil hard to setting point, remove mint, and pour into small hot jars. Eat with roast lamb.

Orange Jelly

> 1 pint orange juice
> Juice of 2 lemons
> ½ pint water
> 1¾ lb sugar

Strain the orange and lemon juice and boil with the water for 10 minutes. Stir in the sugar until dissolved. Boil hard to setting point and pour into hot jars.

Orange & Apple Jelly

> 4 sweet oranges
> 3 lb cooking apples
> 3¼ pints water

Cut the oranges and apples into pieces without peeling and coring or removing pith. Simmer in the water for 1½ hours until the fruit and peel are tender. Strain through a jelly bag and measure the juice. Allow 1 lb sugar to each pint of juice. Heat the juice gently, stirring in the sugar until dissolved. Boil hard to setting point and pour into hot jars.

Parsley Jelly

> Parsley
> Sugar

Wash plenty of fresh parsley including the stalks. Put into a pan and cover with water. Boil for 30 minutes until tender. Strain through a jelly bag and measure the juice. Allow 1 lb sugar to each pint of juice. Heat the juice gently, stirring in the sugar until dissolved. Boil hard to setting point and pour into hot jars.

Plum Jelly

2 lb Victoria plums
½ pint water
Juice of 2 lemons
Sugar

Simmer the plums in the water until soft. Strain through a jelly bag and measure the liquid. Allow 1 lb sugar to each pint of liquid. Add sugar and lemon juice and heat slowly, stirring to dissolve the sugar. Boil hard to setting point. Pour into hot jars.

Plum & Apple Jelly

4 lb ripe red plums
4 lb cooking apples
Sugar

Cut up plums and apples, without peeling and coring. Put into a pan with just enough water to cover and simmer for 1 hour until the fruit is soft. Strain through a jelly bag and measure the juice. Allow 1 lb sugar to each pint of juice. Heat the juice gently, stirring in the sugar until dissolved. Boil hard to setting point and pour into hot jars.

Pomegranate Jelly

6 very ripe pomegranates
Juice of 2 oranges
Juice of 2 lemons
Grated rind of 1 lemon
Sugar

Remove the juice sacs from the pomegranates and mash them to extract the juice. Add the orange and lemon juices and strain. Add an equal amount of water and simmer with the lemon rind for 15 minutes. Add 1 lb sugar to each pint of liquid and boil to setting point. A teaspoon of rose-water may be added if liked. Pour into hot jars and cover.

Raspberry Jelly

Raspberries
Sugar

Simmer raspberries very gently without water. When the fruit is soft, and the juice extracted, strain through a jelly bag, and measure the juice. Allow 1 lb sugar to each pint of juice. Heat the mixture slowly, stirring until the sugar has dissolved. Boil hard to setting point. Pour into small hot jars.

Raspberry & Apple Jelly

4 lb raspberries
2 lb cooking apples
2 pints water
Sugar

Put the raspberries in a pan with the apples which have been cut up without peeling and coring. Add water and simmer for 1 hour until the fruit is soft. Strain through a jelly bag and measure the juice. Allow 1 lb sugar to each pint of juice. Heat the juice gently, stirring in the sugar until dissolved. Boil hard to setting point and pour into hot jars.

Raspberry & Redcurrant Jelly

2 lb raspberries
2 lb redcurrants
1 pint water
Sugar

Put the fruit into the water and simmer gently until the fruit is very soft. Strain through a jelly bag and measure the juice. Allow 1 lb sugar to each pint of juice. Heat the juice gently, stirring in the sugar until dissolved. Boil hard to setting point, and pour into small hot jars. This makes an excellent glaze for cakes and flans.

Redcurrant Jelly

3 lb redcurrants
1 pint water
Sugar

Put the redcurrants on their stalks into a pan with the water. Simmer gently until the fruit is very soft. Strain through a jelly bag and measure the juice. Allow 1 lb sugar to each pint of juice. Stir until the sugar has dissolved. Boil hard to setting point. This jelly sets very quickly and should be potted up as soon as it is ready. Pour into small hot jars. Eat with roast lamb or mutton, or with hare or game.

Spiced Redcurrant Jelly

3 lb redcurrants
1 pint water
¼ pint white vinegar
3 cloves
½ stick cinnamon
Sugar

Simmer the redcurrants with the water and vinegar. Put the spices in a muslin bag and suspend in the pan. When the fruit is soft, remove the spice bag. Strain through a jelly bag and measure the juice. Allow 1 lb sugar to each pint of juice. Heat the juice gently, stirring in the sugar until dissolved. Boil hard to setting point and pour into hot jars. This is excellent with roast lamb or with game.

Rhubarb Jelly

3 lb rhubarb
1½ lb cooking apples
3 pints water
3 lemons
Sugar
Ground ginger or cinnamon (optional)

Cut up the rhubarb and put into a pan with the apples which have been cut up without peeling and coring. Add water and the grated rind and juice of the lemons. Simmer for 1 hour until the fruit is soft. Strain through a jelly bag and measure the juice. Allow 1 lb sugar to each pint of juice. Heat the juice gently, stirring in the sugar until dissolved. Boil hard to setting point and pour into hot jars. A little ground ginger or cinnamon may be added during the final cooking if liked.

Rose Hip Jelly

1 lb rose hips
2 lb cooking apples
1 pint water
Lemon juice
Sugar

Simmer rose hips in ½ pint water. Cut up apples without peeling and coring and simmer in remaining water. Strain both fruits through separate jelly bags. Mix the liquids and measure them. Allow the juice of 1 lemon and 1 lb sugar to each pint of liquid. Stir over low heat until the sugar has dissolved. Boil hard to setting point and pour into hot jars.

Rowanberry Jelly

4 lb rowanberries
4 tablespoons lemon juice
1½ pints water
Sugar

Use ripe rowanberries. Remove from stems and put into pan with the lemon juice and water. Simmer for 45 minutes until the fruit is soft. Strain through a jelly bag and measure the juice. Allow 1 lb sugar to each pint of juice. Heat the juice gently, stirring in the sugar until dissolved. Boil hard to setting point and pour into hot jars. This jelly is good with venison, game and roast lamb or mutton.

Sloe Jelly

2 lb sloes
Sugar

Prick the sloes, cover with water and simmer until tender. Strain through a jelly bag and measure the juice. Allow 1 lb sugar to each pint of juice. Heat the juice gently, stirring in the sugar until dissolved. Boil hard to setting point and pour into hot jars.

Sloe & Apple Jelly

1 lb sloes
6 lb cooking apples
Peel of 2 lemons
Sugar

Put sloes in a pan with apples which have been cut up without peeling and coring. Add the lemon rind and just enough water to cover and simmer for 1 hour until the apples are tender. Strain through a jelly bag and measure the juice. Allow 1 lb sugar to each pint of juice. Heat the juice gently, stirring in the sugar until dissolved. Boil hard to setting point and pour into hot jars.

Strawberry Jelly

2 lb strawberries
Juice of 1 lemon
Sugar

Heat strawberries very gently with the lemon juice until the juice runs and the fruit is soft. Strain through a jelly bag and measure the juice. Allow 1 lb sugar to each pint of juice. Heat the juice gently, stirring in the sugar until dissolved. Boil hard to setting point and pour into hot jars.

Strawberry & Redcurrant Jelly

      1 lb strawberries
      8 oz redcurrants
      4 tablespoons water
      Sugar

Put strawberries and redcurrants into a pan with water. Simmer until soft. Strain through a jelly bag and measure the juice. Allow 1 lb sugar to each pint of juice. Heat the juice gently, stirring in the sugar until dissolved. Boil hard to setting point and pour into hot jars.

Wild Strawberry Jelly

      $2\frac{1}{2}$ lb wild (or Alpine) strawberries
      Juice of 1 lemon
      1 pint water
      Sugar

Put the strawberries into a pan with lemon juice and water. Bring slowly to the boil and simmer for 10 minutes. Strain through a jelly bag and measure the juice. Allow 1 lb sugar to each pint of juice. Heat the juice gently, stirring in the sugar until dissolved. Boil hard to setting point and pour into hot jars.

Tomato Jelly

      3 lb ripe tomatoes
      $1\frac{1}{2}$ lb sugar
      3 tablespoons lemon juice
      1 small cinnamon stick

Cut the tomatoes in pieces and simmer them very gently until soft. Strain through a jelly bag. Heat the juice with the lemon juice and cinnamon stick and stir in sugar until dissolved. Boil hard to setting point. Remove the cinnamon stick and pour into small hot jars. This can be eaten as a spread, or with ham or poultry, or with cream cheese.

Whitecurrant Jelly

> 3 lb whitecurrants
> 1 pint water
> Sugar

Pick the whitecurrants from their stalks and simmer gently in water until soft. Strain through a jelly bag and measure the juice. Allow 1 lb sugar to each pint of juice. Heat the juice gently, stirring in the sugar until dissolved. Boil hard to setting point and pour into hot jars.

Autumn Jelly

> 1 lb cooking apples
> 1 lb quinces
> 8 oz cranberries
> Sugar

Cut the apples and quinces in pieces without peeling and coring. Put into a pan with the cranberries and just cover with water. Simmer for 1 hour until the fruit is soft. Strain through a jelly bag and measure the juice. Allow 1 lb sugar to each pint of juice. Heat the juice gently, stirring in the sugar until dissolved. Boil hard to setting point and pour into hot jars.

Four Fruit Jelly

- 1 lb redcurrants
- 1 lb raspberries
- 1 lb strawberries
- 1 lb black cherries
- 1 teaspoon tartaric acid
- 1 pint water
- Sugar

Use firm fruit which is just ripe. Put all the fruit into a pan with the acid and water. Simmer until the fruit is soft. Strain through a jelly bag and measure the juice. Allow 1 lb sugar to each pint of juice. Heat the juice gently, stirring in the sugar until dissolved. Boil hard to setting point and pour into hot jars. This jelly is very good for pastries and tarts.

CHAPTER FIVE
Marmalades

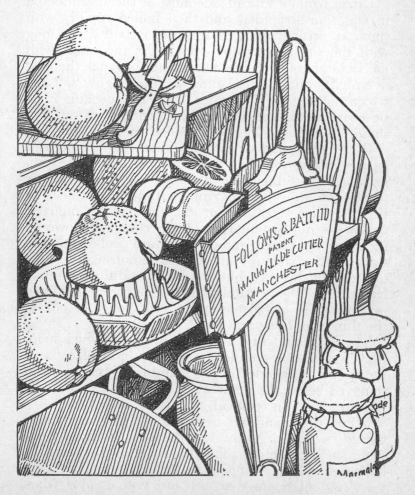

This chapter concerns marmalade made with citrus fruit. The term 'marmalade' also applies to a thick fruit and sugar purée which sets to a firm paste and is used in a number of dishes, but the method of preparation is obviously different from that of the traditional breakfast preserve. Recipes for soft fruit and stone fruit marmalades are therefore included in Chapter Three JAMS.

Citrus fruit for marmalade must be sliced, simmered in water until tender, and then boiled rapidly with sugar to setting point. If the peel is boiled too long with the sugar, a syrupy preserve is the result with hard chunks of peel. It is not essential to soak the fruit overnight, but the peel must be thoroughly soft between the fingers. The water in the first cooking must be evaporated, and usually the contents of the pan should be reduced by about half to ensure a good set.

Cutting up the fruit can be exhausting. If the fruit is very pithy, the skin must be peeled off, the pith removed, and then the peel sliced. Sweet oranges which are thin-skinned can be time-savers because their cutting is easy. Cut the oranges in quarters *lengthways*, put two quarters together flat side down on the chopping board, and cut fruit and peel together in thin or thick strips. Thin-skinned lemons can also be quickly cut this way, but grapefruit and thick-skinned lemons need the de-pithing treatment. Even if chunky marmalade is being made, the peel should be cut on the thin side, because it swells in cooking.

The pips and white pith contain pectin which helps the set of the marmalade, so they should be placed in a muslin bag suspended in the pan during cooking, and removed before the sugar is added. The bag should be well squeezed on removal, to extract all liquid.

When the sugar has been added, the marmalade should be stirred gently over low heat to dissolve the sugar before boiling. The mixture should then be boiled quickly to setting point. When a little poured on to a cold plate starts to set and will wrinkle when pushed with a finger, the marmalade is ready. It should be cooled slightly before potting, and stirred well to prevent the peel rising in the jars. Clean warm jars should be filled right to the top and covered with a wax circle. The marmalade may be covered at once or when completely cold.

Carrot & Orange Marmalade

2 sweet oranges
1 lemon
2 lb carrots
1 pint water
2 lb sugar

Squeeze the juice from the oranges and the lemon. Shred the peel finely and soak in the water overnight. Cut the carrots into matchstick pieces. Put carrots and peel into a pan, with the pips suspended in a muslin bag. Simmer 1 hour until the peel is tender. Take out the bag of peel and squeeze out liquid. Stir in the sugar and lemon juice until sugar has dissolved. Boil rapidly to setting point. Cool slightly, stir well, pour into hot jars and cover.

Ginger Marmalade

5 Seville oranges
5 pints water
3 lb cooking apples
6½ lb sugar
8 oz crystallised ginger
½ oz ground ginger

Cut the oranges in half and squeeze out the juice. Shred the peel finely and cut up the flesh. Put the pips and trimmings into a muslin bag in the pan with orange peel and flesh, juice and water. Simmer for 1½ hours, and remove the bag of pips, squeezing all the liquid out. Peel and core the apples and cut them into slices. Simmer in 4 tablespoons water until pulped. Add the apples to the oranges and stir in the sugar until dissolved. Add the ginger cut in pieces and the ground ginger. Boil rapidly to setting point. Cool slightly, stir well, pour into hot jars and cover.

Grapefruit & Lemon Marmalade

> 3 grapefruit
> 4 lemons
> 4 pints water
> 3 lb sugar

Cut the fruit in half and squeeze out the juice, and strain it into a pan. Remove most of the pith and the membranes from the grapefruit, and put with the pips of both fruit into a muslin bag. Shred the grapefruit and lemon peel, and put it with the juice, water and bag of pips into the pan. Simmer until tender. Take out the bag of pips, squeezing out all the liquid. Stir in the sugar until dissolved, and bring the mixture to the boil. Boil rapidly to setting point. Leave to cool for a few minutes, stir well, pour into hot jars and cover.

Lemon Marmalade

> 8 large lemons
> 8 pints cold water
> Sugar

Peel the lemons very thinly and cut the peel into very fine shreds. Put pith and pips into a muslin bag. Cut up the flesh of the lemons. Put fruit, peel and bag of pips into a pan with water and simmer for $1\frac{1}{2}$ hours. Remove bag of pips and squeeze out liquid. Weigh the contents of the pan and add an equal weight of sugar. Stir in sugar until dissolved. Bring to the boil, and boil for 20 minutes. Cool slightly and stir well. Pour into jars and cover.

Lemon Shred Marmalade

5 lemons
1 grapefruit
6 pints water
Sugar

Peel the lemons thinly, and remove white pith. Cut the peel in fine shreds, cover with 1 pint water, and simmer with a lid on until the peel is soft. Cut up the lemon pulp and the grapefruit into small pieces. Cover with remaining water and boil gently with a lid on for $1\frac{1}{2}$ hours until the fruit is soft. Drain the lemon shreds and add the liquid to the fruit pulp. Bring to the boil and strain through a jelly bag. Measure the liquid and allow 1 lb sugar to each pint of liquid. Put sugar, liquid and lemon peel into a pan, and stir until the sugar has dissolved. Boil hard for 15 minutes to setting point. Cool slightly and stir well. Pour into hot jars and cover.

Lime Marmalade

12 limes
3 pints water
3 lb sugar

Peel the limes very thinly and slice the peel finely. Squeeze out the juice. Cut up the fruit pulp and put with the pips into a muslin bag. Put the peel, juice, bag of pips and the water into a pan. Simmer for 1 hour. Remove the bag of pips, squeezing to remove all the liquid. Stir in the sugar until dissolved, and boil rapidly for 10 minutes. Leave to stand for a few minutes, stir well, pour into hot jars and cover.

Orange Jelly Marmalade

2 lb Seville oranges
1 lemon
4 pints water
Sugar

Grate the rind from the oranges and the lemon. Remove all the white from the oranges and the lemon, and cut up the flesh. Put the flesh and grated rinds into a pan with water, bring to the boil, and simmer for 30 minutes. Put through a jelly bag and weigh the liquid. Allow 1 lb sugar to each pint of juice. Stir until sugar has dissolved and boil rapidly to setting point. Pour into hot jars and cover.

Orange Marmalade with Honey

Sweet oranges
Honey

Peel the oranges and shred the peel finely. Cook the peel in a little water until tender, and then drain. Remove the pith and pips from the oranges and measure the orange pulp. To each pint of orange pulp, allow 1 lb honey and 8 oz prepared rinds. Simmer pulp, honey and rinds together gently for 40 minutes, stirring often. Cool slightly, stir well, pour into hot jars and cover.

Sweet Orange & Lemon Marmalade

4 sweet oranges
5 lemons
5 pints water
4 lb sugar

Cut the fruit into thin slices, putting pips into a muslin bag. Cut each slice into quarters. Put fruit, water and bag of pips into a pan and boil gently for 1½ hours. Remove bag of pips and squeeze out liquid.

Stir in sugar until dissolved. Boil hard for 10 minutes. Cool slightly and stir well. Pour into hot jars and cover.

Orange Shred Marmalade

> 2 lb Seville oranges
> 4½ pints water
> Juice of 2 lemons
> 3 lb sugar

Peel enough thin rind from the oranges to weigh 4 oz, and cut into thin strips. Cut up the fruit and put into a pan with 2½ pints water and the lemon juice. Cover and simmer for 2 hours. Simmer the peel in 1 pint water with a lid on until the shreds are soft. Strain the liquid into the fruit pulp. Strain the pulp through a jelly bag and leave to drip for 15 minutes. Simmer the pulp in the remaining water for 20 minutes, and then leave to strain through a jelly bag overnight. Put the two liquids together and stir in the sugar until dissolved. Add the peel and boil hard to setting point. Cool slightly and stir well. Pour into hot jars and cover.

Seville Orange Marmalade (1)

> 2 lb Seville oranges
> 4 pints water
> 1 lemon
> 4 lb sugar

Cut the fruit in half and squeeze out the juice and the pips. Tie the pips in a muslin bag. Slice the peel thinly and put in a pan with the water, juice of the lemon, and the bag of pips. Simmer for about 1½ hours until the peel is soft and the liquid is reduced by half. Remove the bag of pips and squeeze out all the liquid. Stir in the sugar until dissolved. Boil rapidly to setting point. Cool slightly, stir well, pour into hot jars and cover.

Seville Orange Marmalade (2)

2 lb Seville oranges
1½ pints water
1½ lb sugar

Put the whole oranges in a pan with the water. Cover and boil 1½ hours until tender. Cool and drain, and save the liquid. Cut the oranges into quarters. Scrape away the pulp and put it through a sieve. Shred the peel finely and add to the pulp, the cooking liquid and the sugar, and dissolve the sugar over low heat. Bring to the boil and boil for about 45 minutes to setting point. Cool slightly, stir well, pour into hot jars and cover.

Seville Orange Marmalade (3)

2 lb Seville oranges
Juice of 1 lemon
3 pints water
3 lb sugar

Put the oranges into water, cover and simmer for 1½ hours until tender. Drain, saving the liquid, and cut up the fruit into slices. Put the pips into the cooking liquid together with the lemon juice and boil for 5 minutes before straining. Add the fruit to the liquid and boil for 5 minutes. Stir in the sugar until dissolved, then bring to the boil and boil rapidly to setting point. Cool slightly, stir well, pour into hot jars and cover.

Seville Orange Marmalade (Dark)

                3 lb Seville oranges
                1 lemon
                5 pints water
                6 lb sugar
                1 tablespoon black treacle

Cut the oranges in half and squeeze out the juice. Put the pips into a muslin bag. Cut the fruit into thick shreds. Put into the pan with juice, the juice of the lemon, water and the bag of pips. Simmer for about 2 hours until the peel is tender. Take out the bag of pips, and squeeze out the liquid. Stir in the sugar and black treacle until dissolved and boil quickly to setting point. Cool slightly, stir well, pour into hot jars and cover. If liked, 4 tablespoons rum or whisky may be added just before pouring into pots.

Old-Fashioned Scotch Marmalade

                2 lb Seville oranges
                4 pints water
                4 lb sugar

Remove the rind from the oranges as thinly as possible and cut it into small pieces (not shreds). Remove all the white pith, and cut the fruit into small pieces. Put the pips into some of the water allowed in the recipe and leave for 12 hours. Cover the fruit and the peel with the rest of the water brought to the boil. Leave to stand for 12 hours. Add the liquid from the pips and simmer for 2 hours until the peel is tender. Stir in the sugar until dissolved. Bring to the boil and boil to setting point. Cool slightly and stir well. Pour into hot jars and cover.

Pineapple & Orange Marmalade

3 sweet oranges
1 lemon
30 oz tin pineapple chunks
4 lb sugar

Shred the oranges and lemon and put in enough water to cover together with the pips tied in a muslin bag. Simmer until tender and remove the bag of pips. Add the finely cut pineapple with juice and simmer for 15 minutes. Stir in the sugar until dissolved and boil rapidly for 30 minutes. Cool slightly, stir well, pour into hot jars and cover.

Tangerine Marmalade

$2\frac{1}{4}$ lb tangerines
1 medium grapefruit
1 lemon
5 pints water
$\frac{1}{4}$ oz tartaric acid
3 lb sugar

Peel the tangerines, cut the peel into fine shreds and tie it in a muslin bag. Peel the grapefruit and lemon and put through the mincer. Cut up all the fruit flesh and put into a pan with the peels, the water and the acid. Simmer for 30 minutes and remove the tangerine peel. Continue simmering for $1\frac{1}{2}$ hours. Wash the tangerine peel in a sieve in cold water and drain well. Strain the pulp through a jelly bag and return the juice to the pan. Bring to the boil and stir in the sugar until it dissolves. Add the tangerine peel and boil quickly to setting point. Skim and cool slightly. Stir well, pour into hot jars and cover.

Tangerine & Lemon Marmalade

6 tangerines
4 lemons
3½ pints water
3½ lb sugar

Shred the tangerine and lemon peels very finely. Tie the pith and pips into a muslin bag. Cut up the fruit into small pieces. Put the peel, fruit and water into a pan with the muslin bag of pips. Bring to the boil, and boil until the peel is soft and the fruit mixture is thick. Remove the muslin bag and squeeze out liquid. Stir in the sugar until dissolved, and boil hard for 10 minutes. Cool slightly and stir well. Pour into hot jars and cover.

Tangerine & Lime Marmalade

9 tangerines
3 limes
2½ pints water
1½ lb sugar

Squeeze juice from the tangerines and limes. Slice the fruit as finely as possible and put pips into a muslin bag. Put fruit juice and water into a pan, and suspend the muslin bag. Bring to the boil and simmer for 1¼ hours until the peel is soft. Stir in the sugar until dissolved. Boil rapidly for about 5 minutes. Cool slightly, stir well, pour into hot jars and cover.

Three Fruit Marmalade

2 grapefruit
2 sweet oranges
4 lemons
6 pints water
6 lb sugar

Cut all the fruit in half. Put the pips, and the pith and membranes from the grapefruit into a muslin bag. Shred all peel finely and cut up the flesh roughly. Put the peel, flesh, water and bag of pips into a pan and simmer for 1½ hours. Take out the bag of pips and squeeze to extract the liquid. Stir in the sugar until dissolved, and boil rapidly to setting point. Cool slightly and stir well. Pour into hot jars and cover.

Four Fruit Marmalade

> 2 apples
> 2 sweet oranges
> 2 lemons
> 1 grapefruit
> Sugar

Peel and core the apples. Cut oranges, lemons and grapefruit in half and take out pips. Put apple peel, cores and fruit pips into a muslin bag. Chop the apples and shred the citrus fruit finely. Weigh the fruit and allow 1 pint water to each lb fruit. Put fruit, water and bag of pips into pan and boil gently for 1½ hours. Take out the bag of pips and squeeze out the liquid. Measure the fruit mixture and allow 1 lb sugar to each pint of pulp. Warm the sugar and add to the fruit. Stir until dissolved and then boil rapidly to setting point. Cool slightly and stir well. Pour into hot jars and cover.

Pressure-Cooker Marmalade

> 2 lb Seville oranges
> Juice of 2 lemons
> 2 pints water
> 4 lb sugar

Peel the oranges thinly and cut peel into thin strips. Remove the pith and put into a muslin bag with the pips. Cut up the fruit roughly. Put fruit, peel, lemon juice and muslin bag of pips into the pressure cooker with 1 pint water. Bring to 10 lb pressure and cook for 10 minutes. Leave to cool and reduce the pressure at room temperature. Remove bag of pips and squeeze out liquid. Add the remaining water and sugar to the pan and heat gently until the sugar dissolves. Bring to the boil and boil hard to setting point. Cool slightly and stir well. Pour into hot jars and cover.

Blender Chunky Marmalade

> 2 lb Seville oranges
> 1 lemon
> 4 pints water
> 4 lb sugar

Cut fruit in quarters and take out pips, tying them in a muslin bag. Blend fruit with some of the water on high speed until well chopped. Pour into preserving pan, and continue until all fruit is used. Add remaining water, and boil for 1 hour. Take out bag of pips. Stir in sugar over gentle heat until it has dissolved. Boil rapidly to setting point. Cool slightly, stir well, and pour into warm jars.

Blender Jelly Marmalade

> 8 Seville oranges
> 2 sweet oranges
> 2 lemons
> 8 pints water
> 7 lb sugar

Cut oranges and lemons into pieces, removing pips and tying them in a muslin bag. Blend oranges and lemons with water until just chopped. Add remaining water and leave to stand overnight. Boil for 30 minutes and strain through muslin. Add 1 lb sugar to each pint of juice. Heat gently until sugar has dissolved, and boil vigorously to setting point, which will take about 45 minutes. Pour into warm jars.

Blender Three Fruit Marmalade

> 1 grapefruit
> 1 sweet orange
> 2 lemons
> 3 pints water
> 3 lb sugar

Peel grapefruit and scrape off white pith. Cut fruit and peel into pieces. Cut orange and lemons into pieces and take out pips. Tie pips in a muslin bag. Blend fruit and water until chopped. Add remaining water and cook gently until the peel is soft and with water reduced by half. Remove pips. Stir in sugar over low heat until dissolved, then boil rapidly to setting point. Cool slightly, stir and pour into warm jars.

Blender Jelly Shred Marmalade

> 1½ lb lemons
> 3 pints water
> 3 lb sugar

Remove rind from fruit, and shred 6 oz rind thinly. Put shreds loosely in a muslin bag. Cut fruit in pieces and blend with water until chopped. Add remaining water, and bag containing shreds. Cook gently until fruit is soft and water reduced by half. Drain bag of shreds without squeezing. Strain pulp and return to pan with liquid drained from the shreds. Bring to boil, add sugar and stir until dissolved. Add shreds, and boil rapidly to setting point. Remove scum, cool for a few minutes, and stir before pouring into warm jars.

CHAPTER SIX
Jams, Jellies and Marmalades made with Commercial Pectin

Pectin is an essential ingredient for a good 'set' in jams, jellies and marmalades. When pectin is not present in some fruit, or when supplies of home-made pectin (in the form of apple or gooseberry juice, for instance) are not to hand, use may successfully be made of bottled commercial pectin.

This pectin speeds up the process of jam-making, and guarantees a successful jam which retains the natural goodness, flavour and colour of the fruit. There are no general rules for using this pectin, as each recipe is different, but firm ripe fruit should be used, and all ingredients weighed carefully. A really large pan should be used so that a full rolling boil can be achieved quickly. The jam should be stored in a cool, dry place.

Many people have learned to rely on commercial pectin for making successful strawberry jam, but there are many other delicious recipes which can be confidently made in this way. Further recipes using commercial pectin are included in Chapter Thirteen (FREEZER JAMS).

Apple & Quince Jam

> 3 lb cooking apples
> 3 lb quinces
> $\frac{1}{2}$ pint water
> $6\frac{1}{2}$ lb sugar
> 6 tablespoons lemon juice
> 1 bottle Certo

Peel and core the apples and cut into small pieces. These should then weigh 2 lb. Peel and core the quinces and chop as finely as possible. Put fruit into large saucepan with the water, bring to the boil, cover and simmer for 30 minutes. Measure $4\frac{1}{2}$ lb prepared fruit and juice into a preserving pan. Add the sugar and lemon juice. Heat slowly until the sugar has dissolved, stirring occasionally. Bring to a full rolling boil and boil rapidly for 2 minutes. Remove from the heat and stir in the Certo. Skim, pot and cover.

Crushed Pineapple & Dried Apricot Jam

$\frac{1}{4}$ lb dried apricots
$\frac{3}{4}$ pt water
1 lemon
16 oz can crushed pineapple
3 lb sugar
$\frac{1}{2}$ bottle Certo

Cut up the dried apricots, and put to soak in the water with the thinly pared lemon rind and the juice of the lemon. Leave for 24 hours. Put the apricots and liquid into a preserving pan, and the crushed pineapple and sugar. Heat slowly, stirring occasionally, until the sugar has dissolved. Bring to a full rolling boil and boil hard for 1 minute. Remove from the heat, and stir in Certo. Leave to cool for 10–15 minutes to prevent fruit floating. Skim, pot and cover.

Dried Apricot Jam

$\frac{1}{2}$ lb dried apricots
$1\frac{1}{2}$ pints water
3 tablespoons lemon juice
3 lb sugar
1 bottle Certo

Wash the fruit and leave to soak for at least 4 hours in the water. Simmer in a covered pan for about 30 minutes to break up the fruit. Measure into a pan $1\frac{1}{2}$ pints prepared fruit pulp, making up the amount if necessary, with water. Add the lemon juice and sugar, heat gently, stirring occasionally until the sugar has dissolved. Bring to a full rolling boil and boil rapidly for 1 minute, stirring occasionally. Remove from the heat and stir in the Certo. Skim if necessary. Pot and cover.

Greengage & Almond Preserve

2½ lb greengages
2 oz chopped almonds
½ pint water
3 tablespoons lemon juice
3¼ lb sugar
½ bottle Certo

Wash the fruit and put in a pan with water and lemon juice. Bring to the boil, cover and simmer for 15 minutes, stirring occasionally. Add sugar and almonds and heat gently, stirring until the sugar has dissolved. Bring to a full rolling boil and boil rapidly for 1 minute stirring occasionally. Remove from heat and stir in the Certo. Skim if necessary and remove some of the stones. Allow to cool to prevent fruit floating. Pot and cover.

Greengage & Benedictine Jam

2½ lb greengages
9 fluid oz water
1 fluid oz Benedictine
3 tablespoons lemon juice
3¼ lb sugar
½ bottle Certo

Wash the fruit and put in a pan with the water and lemon and Benedictine. Bring to the boil, cover and simmer for 15 minutes, stirring occasionally. Add the sugar and heat gently, stirring until the sugar has dissolved. Bring to a full rolling boil and boil rapidly for 1 minute stirring occasionally. Remove from the heat and stir in the Certo. Skim if necessary and remove some of the stones. Allow to cool to prevent the fruit floating. Pot and cover.

Lemon & Blackcurrant Jam

2 lb blackcurrants
½ pint water
3 teaspoons grated lemon peel
3¼ lb sugar
½ bottle Certo

Top, tail and wash the fruit. Crush well and put the fruit into a large pan with the water and lemon peel and bring to the boil. Simmer covered for 15 minutes, or until the skins are soft.

Add the sugar, stir well and heat gently until the sugar has dissolved. Bring to a full rolling boil and boil rapidly for 1 minute, stirring occasionally. Remove from heat and stir in Certo. Skim if necessary. Pot and cover.

Marrow & Ginger Jam

1 large marrow (approx. 3 lb)
4 tablespoons water
3¼ lb sugar
2 tablespoons lemon juice
2 oz bruised root ginger
4 oz chopped crystallised ginger
1 bottle Certo

Peel the marrow, discarding skin and seeds, and cut up finely. Place the marrow in a pan with the water and simmer, covered, for 20 minutes. Root ginger should be tied in a muslin bag and placed in a pan together with sugar, cooked marrow, chopped crystallised ginger and lemon juice; mix well and heat gently stirring occasionally, until the sugar has dissolved. Bring to a full rolling boil for 2 minutes. Remove from the heat, take out the muslin bag and stir in the Certo. Allow to cool to prevent fruit floating. Pot and cover.

Orange Blossom Raspberry Jam

        4 lb raspberries
        5½ lb sugar
        1 bottle Certo
        2 teaspoons orange essence

Crush the berries and place in a pan with the sugar. Heat gently, stirring occasionally, until the sugar has dissolved. Bring quickly to a full rolling boil and boil rapidly for 2 minutes stirring at intervals. Remove from heat and stir in the Certo and orange essence. Skim if necessary. Allow to cool to prevent the fruit from floating. Pot and cover.

Peach Jam

        2 lb peaches
        3 tablespoons lemon juice
        1 pint water
        3 lb sugar
        ½ bottle Certo

Peel and stone the peaches and cut into slices. Put into pan with lemon juice and water. Bring to the boil and simmer gently with a lid on until fruit is tender. Add sugar and stir until dissolved. Bring to boil and boil rapidly for 2 minutes. Add Certo and stir. Cool to prevent fruit floating. Pot and cover.

Pear & Ginger Jam

        3 lb ripe Conference pears
        3¼ lb sugar
        4 oz crystallised ginger
        1 bottle Certo

Peel and core pears. Crush completely (a liquidiser can be used). Put the sugar and fruit into a large saucepan or preserving pan and mix well. Place on low heat and stir until sugar has dissolved. Add

88

chopped ginger and bring gradually to a full rolling boil. Boil hard for 2 to 3 minutes, stirring at intervals. Remove from heat and stir in Certo. Stir and skim alternately for 3 minutes. Pot and cover.

Plum & Apple Sherry Jam

$2\frac{1}{2}$ lb plums
3 lb cooking apples
$\frac{1}{4}$ pint sherry
$\frac{1}{4}$ pint water
$6\frac{3}{4}$ lb sugar
1 bottle Certo

Wash the plums, cut into pieces, removing as many of the stones as desired. Peel and core the apples, cut into small pieces. Put the fruit, water and sherry into a large saucepan, bring to the boil, cover and simmer for 15 minutes or until the fruit is tender. Add the sugar, stir until dissolved, then bring to a full rolling boil. Boil hard for 2 minutes. Remove from the heat and stir in the Certo. Skim, pot and cover.

Plum Jam with Walnuts & Brandy

5 lb plums
9 fluid oz water
1 fluid oz brandy
$6\frac{1}{2}$ lb sugar
2 oz walnuts—chopped finely
$\frac{1}{2}$ bottle Certo

Wash the plums and cut into pieces, removing as many of the stones as desired. Put fruit, water and brandy into a large pan. If the fruit is very ripe or sweet, add the juice of one lemon. Bring to the boil and simmer covered for 15 minutes, stirring occasionally.

Add the sugar and walnuts and heat gently, stirring until the sugar has dissolved. Bring to a full rolling boil and boil rapidly for 3 minutes, stirring at intervals.

Remove from the heat and stir in the Certo. Skim if necessary. Allow to cool to prevent fruit floating. Pot and cover.

Rhubarb & Raspberry Jam with Port

$1\frac{1}{2}$ lb prepared rhubarb
$\frac{1}{2}$ lb raspberries
3 lb sugar
1 tablespoon water
2 tablespoons Port
1 bottle Certo

Wash the rhubarb and slice or chop finely, but do not peel. Put the sugar into a preserving pan and add the prepared rhubarb and crushed raspberries together with the water and port. Mix well and bring to a full rolling boil, stirring all the time. Boil hard for 3 minutes. Remove from heat and stir in the Certo. Skim if necessary. Pot and cover.

Spiced Gooseberry Jam

4 lb gooseberries
$\frac{1}{2}$ pint water
$6\frac{1}{2}$ lb sugar
$\frac{1}{2}$ teaspoon nutmeg
$\frac{1}{2}$ teaspoon cinnamon
1 bottle Certo

Top, tail and wash the gooseberries. Put them in a large preserving pan and add the water. Bring to the boil and simmer covered for 15 minutes or until the skins are soft, stirring occasionally.

Add sugar and spices and heat slowly until dissolved, stirring at intervals. Bring to a full rolling boil quickly. Boil rapidly for 2 minutes stirring occasionally.

Remove from heat and stir in Certo. Skim if necessary. Allow to cool slightly, pot and cover.

Tawny Port & Damson Jam

2½ lb damsons
3 tablespoons lemon juice
8 fluid oz water
2 fluid oz Tawny Port
3¾ lb sugar
½ bottle Certo

Wash the fruit and put in a pan with the water and lemon juice and the port. Bring to the boil, cover and simmer for 15 minutes, stirring occasionally. Add the sugar and heat gently, stirring occasionally until the sugar has dissolved. Bring to a full rolling boil and boil rapidly for 1 minute, while stirring. Remove from the heat and stir in the Certo. Skim if necessary and remove some of the stones. Allow to cool to prevent fruit floating. Pot and cover.

Whole Strawberry Jam

2¼ lb small strawberries
3 tablespoons lemon juice
3 lb sugar
1 small knob of butter
½ bottle Certo

Hull the fruit and put in a pan with lemon juice and sugar, and stand for 1 hour, stirring occasionally. Place over low heat and heat slowly until the sugar has dissolved, stirring occasionally. Add butter to reduce foaming. Bring to a full rolling boil and boil rapidly for 4 minutes, stirring occasionally. Remove from heat and stir in Certo. Cool for at least 20 minutes to prevent the fruit floating. Pot and cover.

Apple & Damson Jelly

3 lb apples
4 lb damsons
2 pints water
6½ lb sugar
1 bottle Certo

Use only fully ripe fruit. Remove blossom and stem ends of apples and cut into small pieces, do not peel or core. Crush damsons thoroughly but do not peel or stone. Mix and add water, bring to the boil and simmer covered for 20 minutes. Crush with masher and simmer for further 10 minutes.

Place the fruit in jelly bag and leave to drip. Put the sugar and 4½ lb juice into a preserving pan. Heat gently, stirring occasionally until the sugar has dissolved. Bring to boil and add the Certo, stirring constantly. Bring to a full rolling boil and boil hard for 1 minute. Skim, pot and cover.

Blackberry Jelly

3 lb blackberries
¾ pint water
3 tablespoons lemon juice
3¼ lb sugar
1 bottle Certo

Crush fruit thoroughly and simmer gently with water for 10-15 minutes until tender. Strain through a jelly bag and measure juice into a pan. If necessary make up to 2 pints with water. Add the sugar and lemon juice. Heat gently, stirring occasionally until sugar has dissolved. Bring quickly to a full rolling boil. Boil rapidly for 2 minutes. Stir in the Certo and continue boiling for 1 minute, stirring occasionally. Remove from the heat. Skim if necessary. Pot and cover.

Cinnamon Apple Jelly

6 lb cooking apples
3 pints water
6½ lb sugar
½ teaspoon cinnamon
1 small knob of butter
1 bottle Certo

Remove the blossom and stem ends from fruit and cut apples in small pieces. Do not peel or core. Add water, cover and simmer until the fruit is tender. Place the fruit in a jelly cloth or bag and allow to drain. Measure sugar and cinnamon and 4 pints juice into a large preserving pan and mix well. Heat slowly, stirring occasionally, until the sugar has dissolved and add a small piece of butter. Add the Certo, stirring constantly and then bring to a full rolling boil and boil hard for 1 minute. Remove from heat and skim, pot and cover.

Elderberry & Ginger Jelly

4 lb elderberries
¼ pint water
½ oz bruised root ginger
Juice of 2 lemons
2 oz crystallised ginger
3¼ lb sugar
1 bottle Certo

Wash and drain the fruit, place in a saucepan and crush thoroughly. Add the bruised root ginger in a muslin bag, and simmer until tender, about 15 minutes. Strain through a jelly bag and measure the juice into a pan. If necessary make up to two pints with water.

Add the sugar, lemon juice and chopped crystallised ginger and heat gently, stirring occasionally until the sugar has dissolved. Bring quickly to the boil, stir in the Certo and boil hard for 1 minute. Remove from the heat, skim if necessary, allow to cool slightly, pot and cover.

Gooseberry, Apple & Ginger Jelly

> 3 lb apples
> 3 lb gooseberries
> 3¼ pints water
> 1 teaspoon ground ginger
> 6½ lb sugar
> 1 bottle Certo
> Green colouring (optional)

Remove the blossom and stem ends from the apples and cut into small pieces, but do not peel or core them. Wash the gooseberries (no need to top or tail them). Put the gooseberries and apples in a large saucepan with the water and ginger and simmer covered for 20 minutes or until the fruit is soft enough to crush. Strain through a jelly bag and measure the juice into a pan. If necessary make up to four pints with water.

Add the sugar and heat gently stirring occasionally until the sugar has dissolved. Stir in the Certo, bring to a full rolling boil and boil rapidly for 1 minute. Remove from heat, skim and stir in the colouring if desired. Pot and cover.

Mint Jelly

> A large bunch of mint (approx. 2 oz)
> ½ pint white vinegar
> 1 lb sugar
> 1 bottle Certo
> Green colouring

Wash the mint thoroughly and divide in two halves. Take the leaves from one bunch, squeeze out the surplus water and chop finely. Put the vinegar and sugar into a saucepan with the second bunch of mint and stir

over a low heat until the sugar has dissolved. Remove
the bunch of mint. Bring to the boil for 1 minute.

Strain the syrup through muslin and return to the
saucepan. Stir in the Certo, bring to the boil and boil
for 2 minutes. Add the chopped mint and colouring.
Allow to cool slightly to prevent mint floating. Skim,
put into small pots, and cover.

Nutty Currant Jelly

>3 lb blackcurrants
>4 lb redcurrants
>2 pints water
>6 lb sugar
>1 bottle Certo
>2 oz hazelnuts, chopped finely

Wash the fruit and crush thoroughly. Put the currants
in a pan, add the water and bring to the boil. Simmer
covered for 10 minutes, or until the skins are soft.
Strain through a jelly bag and measure the juice into
a pan. If necessary make up to 4 pints with water.

Add the sugar and the chopped nuts and heat
slowly stirring occasionally, until the sugar has
dissolved. Bring to a full rolling boil and boil rapidly
for 1 minute. Add Certo and continue boiling for $\frac{1}{2}$
minute. Remove from heat, skim if necessary. Pot and
cover.

Sweet Cider Jelly

>1 quart sweet apple cider
>$3\frac{1}{4}$ lb sugar
>1 bottle Certo

Measure cider and sugar into large saucepan and
mix. Bring to a boil over hottest flame and at once add
Certo, stirring constantly. Bring to full rolling boil and

boil hard for 1 minute. Remove from flame, skim, pour quickly into pots and cover.

Orange & Ginger Marmalade

    3 lb oranges
    2 lemons
    1½ pints water
    1 level teaspoon bicarbonate soda
    4¾ lb sugar
    4 oz crystallised ginger
    1 small knob of butter
    1 bottle Certo

Wash the fruit and remove the skins. Shave off and discard about half of the white part. Shred the rind very finely and place in a pan with the water and bicarbonate soda. Bring to the boil. Simmer, covered, for about 10 minutes or until the skins can be crushed easily between the thumb and forefinger, stirring occasionally. Cut the peeled fruit, discarding the pips and tough skin, and add fruit and juice to the cooked rind. Simmer, covered, for a further 20 minutes. Put the sugar and 3 pints of prepared fruit into a pan making up the quantity with water if necessary, then add the chopped crystallised ginger and sugar. Heat gently, stirring at intervals until the sugar has dissolved. Add a small knob of butter, bring to a full rolling boil and boil rapidly for 5 minutes. Remove from heat and stir in bottle of Certo. Skim and stir alternately for 7 minutes to cool and prevent the fruit floating. Pot and cover.

Orange Jelly Marmalade

    2 pints canned orange juice
    3½ lb sugar
    1 bottle Certo

Put the orange juice and sugar into a large saucepan. Heat gently, stirring until the sugar has dissolved. Bring to a full rolling boil, stir in the Certo and boil rapidly for 1 minute. Skim, cool slightly, then pot and cover.

Banana Butter

> 10 bananas
> $2\frac{3}{4}$ lb sugar
> Juice of 1 lemon
> $\frac{1}{4}$ teaspoon butter
> 1 bottle Certo

Use only ripe bananas and crush to a fine pulp. Measure sugar, $1\frac{1}{2}$ lb prepared fruit, lemon juice and butter into a large preserving pan. Heat slowly until sugar has dissolved, stirring constantly. Bring quickly to a full rolling boil and boil rapidly for 1 minute. Remove from heat and stir in Certo. Pour quickly into pots and cover.

CHAPTER SEVEN
Curds and Honeys

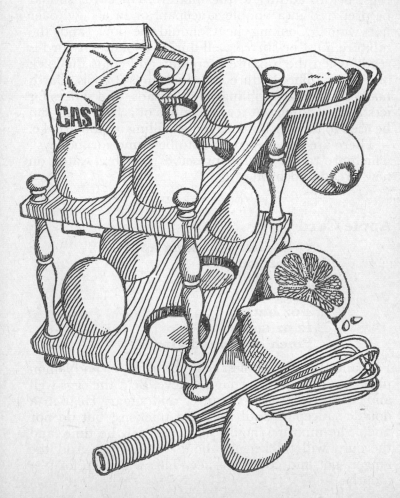

Curds are creamy, fruit-flavoured mixtures of eggs, butter and sugar. Because of their ingredients, storage life is short (usually 1–2 months), and curds are best made in small quantities and stored in small jars, which should be kept in a cool, dark place.

Curds should be made with cube or caster sugar, and with fresh (unsalted) butter. For perfection, fruit juices should be strained, as should the beaten eggs, before adding to the mixture. All curds should be prepared in a double saucepan, or in a bowl over hot water. Cooking heat should be low, and the mixture must be stirred well during cooking. A curd is ready when the mixture is creamy and coats the back of a spoon. The mixture will thicken as it cools. Curds make delicious tart fillings and spreads, and sauces for ices and puddings. A few spoonfuls of a fruit curd can be used to flavour butter icing for filling a sponge cake.

There are very few recipes to be found for 'honeys', which are rather syrupy preserves excellent eaten on new bread and butter.

Apple Curd

> 1½ lb sharp cooking apples
> ¼ pint water
> Juice of 1 lemon
> 2 eggs
> 4 oz butter
> 12 oz sugar
> Pinch of ground ginger

Peel and slice the apples. Simmer in water and lemon juice to a pulp. Put through a sieve. Beat the eggs well and add to the apples, butter and sugar. Heat in a double saucepan until the curd thickens, but do not boil. The mixture should be stirred all the time, and the curd will thicken in about 30 minutes. Add the ginger, pot and cover at once. This will keep for 2–3 months.

Apricot Curd (Dried Fruit)

>   8 oz dried apricots
>   1 lemon
>   2 oz butter
>   8 oz caster sugar
>   2 eggs

Wash the fruit and cover in water. Leave overnight to soak and then cook until soft. Sieve and add to grated rind and juice of the lemon, butter, sugar and well-beaten eggs. Cook in a double saucepan, stirring well, until the curd thickens (about 30 minutes). Pour into hot jars and cover. This will keep 2 months.

Apricot Curd (Fresh Fruit)

>   8 oz fresh apricots
>   1 lemon
>   2 oz butter
>   8 oz caster sugar
>   2 eggs

Put the fruit in a pan with very little water and cook until soft. Sieve and add to grated rind and juice of the lemon, butter, sugar and well-beaten eggs. Cook in a double saucepan, stirring well, until the curd thickens (about 30 minutes). Pour into hot jars and cover. This will keep 2 months.

Blackberry & Apple Curd

>   1 lb apples
>   2 lb blackberries
>   Juice of 2 lemons
>   8 oz butter
>   2½ lb caster sugar
>   4 eggs

Peel and core the apples, and cook with the black-berries in very little water until soft. Put through a sieve. Cook in a double saucepan with lemon juice, butter and sugar. When butter and sugar have melted, add the well-beaten eggs and cook until mixture thickens, stirring well. Pour into hot jars and cover. This will keep 2 months.

Golden Curd

> 2 oz butter
> 2 oranges
> 1 lemon
> 8 oz sugar
> 4 eggs

Melt the butter in the top of a double saucepan. Grate orange and lemon rinds finely, and squeeze out the juice. Put the juice through a strainer. Add grated rinds, juice and sugar to the butter and stir until the sugar dissolves. Cool slightly and stir in well-beaten eggs. Return to heat and cook gently, stirring until the mixture thickens and coats the back of a spoon, which will take about 10 minutes. Pour into hot jars and cover. This will keep 1 month.

Gooseberry Curd

> 3 lb green gooseberries
> $\frac{3}{4}$ pint water
> $1\frac{1}{2}$ lb caster sugar
> 4 oz butter
> 4 eggs

Top and tail the fruit and cook in the water until soft. Put through a sieve. Cook in a double saucepan with the sugar, butter and well-beaten eggs, stirring until the mixture thickens. Pour into hot jars and cover. This will keep 1 month.

Lemon Curd

> 4 large lemons
> 6 oz butter
> 1 lb sugar
> 4 large eggs

Grate the lemon rinds finely, avoiding all pith. Squeeze out the juice and put through a strainer. Melt the butter in a double saucepan, and add lemon rind and juice, sugar and well-beaten eggs. Cook and stir for about 25 minutes until the mixture is smooth and thick. Pour into hot jars and cover. This will keep 2 months.

Rich Lemon Curd

> 4 large lemons
> 6 oz butter
> $1\frac{1}{4}$ lb cube sugar
> 7 eggs

Rub the lemon rinds with cubes of sugar to absorb the lemon oils. Put the sugar with the lemon juice which has been strained, butter and lightly beaten eggs into a double boiler. For perfection, the eggs should also be strained. Cook and stir until the mixture is thick and creamy. Pour into hot jars and cover. This will keep 1 month.

Lemon Curd with Honey

> 4 lemons
> 4 oz butter
> 1 lb clear honey
> 4 eggs and 2 egg yolks

Grate the lemon rinds, and squeeze and strain the juice. Put into a double saucepan with butter and honey. Beat eggs and egg yolks and strain into the mixture. Cook and stir over a gentle heat until thick and creamy. Pour into hot jars and cover. This will keep 2 months.

Orange Curd

3 oranges
1 small lemon
8 oz sugar
5 oz butter
2 eggs

Grate the rinds of the oranges and the lemon. Put the rinds, strained orange and lemon juice, sugar and butter into a double saucepan. Heat until the butter and sugar melt, and stir in well-beaten eggs. Cook and stir until the mixture is thick and creamy. Pour into hot jars and cover. This will keep 2 months.

Orange Curd with Peel

1 large orange
2 oz candied orange peel
4 oz sugar
4 oz butter
3 egg yolks

Grate the orange rind and squeeze and strain the juice. Chop the peel finely. Melt the sugar and butter in a double saucepan. Add the rind and juice, the chopped peel, and the beaten egg yolks. Heat and stir until the mixture thickens. Pour into hot jars and cover. This will keep 2 months. This is a particularly nice filling for tarts.

Raspberry & Apple Curd

$1\frac{1}{2}$ lb raspberries
$3\frac{1}{2}$ lb cooking apples
3 lemons
10 oz butter
$1\frac{3}{4}$ lb sugar
5 eggs
8 fluid oz water

Frozen raspberries may be used for this recipe. They should be thawed and sieved before use. Fresh raspberries should be gently heated until the juices run before sieving. Peel and core the apples, and simmer with grated rind and juice of the lemons until soft. Beat the apple pulp until smooth. Mix apples and raspberries and put into a double saucepan. Add butter, sugar, beaten eggs and water, and cook gently, stirring well, until thick and creamy. Pour into hot jars and cover. This will keep 2 months.

Tangerine Curd

3 tangerines
5 oz sugar
4 oz butter
3 egg yolks

Grate the rind of 2 tangerines finely. Squeeze and strain the juice of all the tangerines. Put rinds, juice, sugar, butter and beaten egg yolks into a double saucepan and cook over a low heat, stirring all the time, until the mixture thickens. Pour into hot jars and cover. This will keep 2 months.

Apple Honey

5 lb apples
2 lb sugar
Grated rind of 1 lemon
1 tablespoon lemon juice
1 oz butter

The best apples are those which "fluff" quickly while cooking. Peel and core the apples and cut into small pieces. Put into a pan with a tight-fitting lid and very little water, and cook gently to a fine pulp. Stir the apples occasionally to prevent burning. Add the sugar, lemon rind and juice, and butter. Bring to the boil, and then simmer for 15 minutes. Pour into hot jars and seal. This will keep for 2-3 months.

Parsley Honey

4 oz fresh parsley
1¼ pints water
1 lb sugar
1 dessertspoon vinegar

Wash the parsley well and chop up roughly, including the stalks. Put into a pan with the water and bring to the boil. Boil gently until the liquid has been reduced to 1 pint. Strain the liquid and put into a clean saucepan with warm sugar. Stir well and when the sugar has dissolved, bring to the boil. Add the vinegar and boil slowly for about 30 minutes until the mixture is like clear honey. Pour into pots and cover.

Tomato Honey

1 lb red tomatoes
1 lb sugar
1 lemon

Chop the tomatoes and put into a pan with the grated rind of the lemon. Simmer until soft, and put mixture through a sieve. Put into the pan with sugar and juice of the lemon, and stir until sugar has dissolved. Boil rapidly until thick. This is a delicious and unusual filling for tarts.

CHAPTER EIGHT
Butters and Cheeses

The terms 'butter' and 'cheese' applied to thick mixtures of fruit pulp and sugar have become somewhat confused, and are now almost interchangeable. Fruit *butters* should be thick and semi-set, of the consistency of thick cream, so that they can be spread. They should be tested on a plate and are ready when no rim of liquid appears round the edge of the mixture. Fruit *cheeses* should be much firmer, and were originally potted into moulds, so that they could be turned out and sliced. They are tested by drawing a spoon across the bottom of the pan until it leaves a clear line. Both preserves should look thick and glossy.

Butters and cheeses are useful to use up large quantities of fruit or windfalls. Quantities are considerably reduced during the cooking process. In general, a butter has half the amount of sugar to fruit pulp; a cheese contains equal quantities of sugar and pulp. If the pulp does not seem very thick, it should be boiled and well-reduced before the sugar is added. Brown sugar gives a good flavour to bland fruits, but darkens the resulting preserve. Powdered spices also tend to darken the preserve, and whole spices tied in muslin may be substituted. A little added lemon juice sharpens and improves the fruit flavours.

Small jars with wide mouths are best for these preserves, particularly if they are to be turned out. The cheeses can be cut in slices to eat with cream or with milk puddings; some of them are also suitable to eat with meat, poultry or game.

Apple Butter

　　6 lb apples
　　2 pints water
　　2 pints cider
　　1 teaspoon ground cloves
　　1 teaspoon ground cinnamon
　　1 teaspoon nutmeg
　　Granulated or soft brown sugar

Do not peel the apples, but cut into large pieces. Simmer in water and cider until soft and put through a sieve. Weigh the pulp and simmer until thick. Add 12 oz sugar to each lb of weighed apples. Stir sugar and spices into apples, and cook gently, stirring frequently, until no surplus liquid remains. Pour into hot jars and cover. This is particularly good made with equal quantities of differently flavoured apples; six different kinds could be used for this recipe. The best apple butter is slightly sharp-flavoured. The same recipe may be used for crabapples.

Apple & Plum Butter

3 lb apples
1 lb plums
Sugar

Peel, core and cut up the apples, and cook in very little water until soft. Stone the plums and add to the apples. Cook until plums are soft. Sieve the mixture and add 12 oz sugar to each lb of pulp. Stir in sugar until dissolved and boil until thick and creamy. Pour into hot jars and cover.

Apricot Cheese (Fresh Fruit)

Fresh apricots
Sugar

Cut the apricots in half and remove stones. Steam the fruit until it is soft. Sieve and add 1 lb of sugar to each pint of pulp. Stir until the sugar has dissolved. Cook and stir until the mixture begins to candy at the edges. Pour into hot jars and cover.

Apricot Cheese (Dried Fruit)

> 1 lb dried apricots
> 1 orange
> 1 lb granulated sugar

Soak the apricots in just enough water to cover overnight. Simmer until very soft. Meanwhile boil the orange until soft. Sieve the apricots and mince the orange. Beat the orange into the apricot pulp. Stir in the sugar until dissolved and boil to setting point. Pour into hot jars and cover.

Black Butter

> Redcurrants
> Blackcurrants
> Gooseberries
> Strawberries
> Sugar

A mixture of some or all of the above fruits can be used. For each 2 lb fruit, allow 1 lb sugar. Prepare and mix the fruits and heat gently in a pan until the juices start to run. Stir in sugar until dissolved, and boil until very thick. Pour into small hot jars and cover. This recipe is about 200 years old and was called 'a nursery preserve'.

Blackberry Cheese

> 4 lb ripe blackberries
> 2 teaspoons citric or tartaric acid
> Sugar

Wash the blackberries and put into a pan with just enough water to cover, and the acid. Bring to the boil, and simmer gently until fruit is soft. Put through a sieve and weigh the pulp. Allow 1 lb sugar to each lb of pulp. Stir in sugar until dissolved, then boil and stir until mixture is thick. Pour into hot jars and cover.

Bullace or Sloe Cheese

4 lb ripe bullaces or sloes
Sugar

Simmer the fruit in very little water until soft. Put through a sieve and weigh the pulp. Allow 1 lb sugar to each lb of pulp. Stir sugar until dissolved, and then boil gently, stirring often for about 1 hour until bright and clear. Pour into hot jars and cover.

Cherry Butter

4 lb cherries
1 lemon
2 lb sugar

Take the stones from the cherries. Remove the kernels from a few of them, blanch and skin. Put the cherries in layers in a bowl with sugar and the grated rind and juice of the lemon. Leave overnight. Simmer for 20 minutes, add kernels and then boil quickly until very thick, stirring well. Pour into small hot jars and cover.

Cherry Cheese

Cherries
Sugar

Take the stones from the cherries. If liked, a few of the kernels can be blanched and skinned and added towards the end of cooking time. Cook the fruit gently without water, and put through a sieve when soft. Weigh the pulp and allow 6 oz sugar to each lb of fruit pulp. Boil the pulp quickly, stirring well, until thick. Stir in sugar until dissolved and boil and stir again until very thick. Pour into small hot jars, adding kernels if liked.

Cranberry Cheese

> 1 lb cranberries
> ½ pint water
> 8 oz sugar

Wash the cranberries and cook them with the water until soft. Put through a sieve and stir in the sugar until dissolved. Cook gently, stirring well, until the mixture is thick and creamy. Pour into small hot jars and cover. This is excellent with cold meat and poultry, and with pancakes.

Damson Cheese

> Damsons
> Sugar

Wash the damsons and just cover with water. Simmer until soft. Put through a sieve and weigh the pulp. Add 12 oz sugar to each pint of damson pulp. Stir the sugar into the pulp until dissolved and then cook and stir for about 45 minutes until the mixture is thick enough to hold the impression of a spoon. Pour into hot jars and cover.

Gooseberry Cheese

> 3 lb green gooseberries
> ½ pint water
> Sugar

Top and tail the gooseberries and simmer in water until soft. Put through a sieve and weigh the pulp. Allow 12 oz sugar to each lb pulp. Stir sugar until dissolved and bring to the boil. Cook gently, stirring all the time, until mixture is thick. Pour into hot jars and cover. This is very good as a spread, or eaten with cold meat, particularly lamb.

Grape Butter

3 lb black grapes
Sugar

Wash fruit and simmer in just enough water to cover until soft. Put through a sieve and weigh the pulp. Allow 8 oz sugar to each lb pulp. Cook pulp until thick, add sugar and stir until dissolved. Bring to the boil, then cook gently, stirring well, until creamy. Pour into hot jars and cover.

Lemon & Apple Butter

4 lb apples
1 lb sugar
Grated rind of 1 lemon

Do not peel the apples. Cut them in pieces and simmer in very little water until soft. Put through a sieve. Add sugar and grated lemon rind, and stir until sugar has dissolved. Cook and stir until thick. Pour into hot jars and cover.

Pear Butter

5 lb cooking pears
$\frac{1}{2}$ pint water
Juice of 1 lemon
Sugar

Do not peel the pears. Cut them into pieces and cook with the water until soft. Sieve the pears and weigh the pulp. Allow 8 oz sugar to each lb pulp. Boil the pulp with the lemon juice until thick. Stir in the sugar until dissolved and bring to the boil. Simmer and stir for about 1 hour until the mixture is thick. Pour into hot jars and cover.

Rhubarb Butter

2 lb rhubarb
4 fluid oz water
1 lb sugar
A little red food colouring

Cut up the rhubarb and cook with the water until tender. Put through a sieve. Bring to the boil, stir in sugar and stir until the sugar has dissolved. Cook and stir until mixture is thick and creamy. Colour to taste with red food colouring, pour into hot jars and cover.

CHAPTER NINE
Conserves and Preserves

The terms 'conserve' and 'preserve' have become a little confused over the years. 'Preserve' is often a word used to describe all types of jams; sometimes it describes a jam with a rather unusual set of ingredients; and sometimes it means a conserve. Originally, a conserve was a fruit preserved whole or sliced in syrup (before the days of fruit bottling). Conserves are meant to be eaten with a spoon as a delicious finish to a meal, rather than spread on bread and butter; generally they are rather richer and sweeter than conventional jams, and more syrupy. A preserve generally sets like jam, but may contain dried fruit, peel, nut kernels, citrus fruit or rind in addition to fresh fruit.

The two words must really now be interchangeable, for they have been confused for so long in handwritten recipes and in cookery books. Whether they are syrupy, or can be turned out like moulds, they make a delicious change from conventional jams, although the ingredients are often almost identical. They may be used with milk puddings, moulds or creams, or ices, and can be eaten alone with cream. Some foreign versions of these jams can be found in Chapter 16 (JAMS FROM ABROAD).

Apple Ginger (1)

> 3 lb apples
> 3 lb sugar
> 1½ pints water
> 1½ oz essence of ginger

Peel and core the apples, and cut them into thick slices. Dissolve the sugar in the water, and bring to a slow boil. Boil for 25 minutes, then drop in the apple slices. Simmer until the apples are yellow and transparent. Stir in essence of ginger and cook for 2 minutes. Lift apple slices into jars, cover with syrup, and seal. Essence of ginger (from the chemists) gives the correct flavour and 'hotness' to this preserve, which is delicious served with cream. It keeps best in screwtop honey or preserving jars.

Apple Ginger (2)

4 lb apples
4 lb sugar
3 pints water
2 oz ground ginger

Peel and core apples and cut them into thin slices. Dissolve the sugar in the water and boil syrup until thick. Add the apple slices and boil until transparent. Stir in ginger, boil for 5 minutes, pour into jars and cover. This is a traditional recipe which is very good for filling tarts.

Apples in Wine

8 lemons
1 pint white wine
4½ lb sugar
5 lb apples
2 tablespoons brandy

Peel the lemons thinly and pour on 1 pint boiling water, and the wine. Leave for 30 minutes. Put lemon peel and liquid into a pan with the juice of the lemons and the sugar. Boil for 10 minutes. Strain the liquid and return to the pan. Peel and core apples, and cut into slices. Simmer until apples are soft and the syrup is thick. Stir in brandy, heat and pour into hot screwtop jars. This is very good served with cream.

Apricot & Lemon Preserve

**1 lb dried apricots
6 pints water
1½ lb lemons
6 lb sugar**

Soak the apricots in half the water overnight. Squeeze the juice from the lemons. Put the pips into a muslin bag, and slice the peel thinly. Put the peel, juice, remaining water, and water from the apricots into a pan, and suspend the pips tied in a bag. Simmer for 1½ hours until the peel is soft. Add the apricots and simmer for 30 minutes. Remove the bag of pips. Stir in the sugar until it dissolves. Bring to the boil, and boil rapidly to setting point. Pour into hot jars and cover.

Banana Preserve

**4½ lb bananas
2 lemons
2 tablespoons rum
Sugar
2 teaspoons ground cinnamon**

Peel and slice the bananas into a bowl. Add the grated rind and the juice of the lemons, and the rum. Toss carefully, and then put bananas in layers with their own weight of sugar. Cover and leave for 24 hours. Put into a pan with cinnamon. Heat gently, stirring until the sugar has dissolved. Bring to the boil, and boil for 5 minutes, stirring all the time. The preserve should be thick and brown. Take off the heat, leave to stand for 10 minutes, pour into jars and cover.

Blackberry & Apple Conserve

2 lb cooking apples
1 lb blackberries
Sugar
1 teaspoon citric acid

Do not peel or core the apples, but cut them into slices. Wash the blackberries. Put apples and blackberries in a pan and cook very gently without water until fruit is tender. Put through a sieve and weigh the purée. Allow 12 oz sugar to each lb of pulp and put into a pan with the citric acid. Simmer for 30 minutes, stirring often, until setting point is reached. Pour into jars and cover. This may be turned out to eat with cream.

Black Cherry Conserve

2 oranges
4 lb black cherries
6 tablespoons lemon juice
2 lb sugar
½ teaspoon ground cinnamon

Slice the oranges very thinly, removing pips. Put into pan and just cover slices with water. Simmer until tender. Stone the cherries. Add cherries, lemon juice, sugar and cinnamon to pan, and stir until sugar has dissolved. Simmer until thick and clear. Pour into hot jars and cover.

Cherry Preserve

4 lb black cherries
2 lb Morello cherries
7 fluid oz lemon juice
3½ lb sugar

Stone black and Morello cherries and mix together with lemon juice and sugar in a bowl. Cover and leave overnight. Put over a low heat and stir gently until sugar has dissolved completely. Bring to a slow boil and simmer about 45 minutes until thick and syrupy. Pour into hot jars and cover.

Cherry & Pineapple Preserve

> 6 lb Morello cherries
> 1 medium pineapple
> 5 lb sugar

Stone the cherries, and shred the pineapple. Put into a pan and simmer for 30 minutes. Add the sugar and stir until dissolved. Bring to the boil, and boil for 20 minutes, stirring well. Pour into hot jars and cover.

Cranberry Orange Conserve

> 1 orange
> $1\frac{1}{4}$ lb cranberries
> $\frac{1}{2}$ pint water
> 12 oz sugar
> 2 oz seedless raisins
> 2 oz chopped walnuts

Cut the orange into very small pieces. Put the orange and the cranberries into the water and simmer for about 40 minutes until soft. Stir in the sugar until it has dissolved. Add the raisins and walnuts. Bring to the boil, stirring well, and simmer for 20 minutes. Pour into hot jars and cover.

Cucumber Conserve

> 4 large cucumbers
> 4 lb sugar
> $2\frac{1}{2}$ oz root ginger

Peel the cucumbers and slice thinly. Cover with the sugar and leave for 24 hours. Strain the juice and sugar into a pan, and simmer gently until the sugar dissolves. Tie the root ginger into a muslin bag and crush it with a heavy weight. Put the bag into the syrup and boil for 45 minutes. Add the cucumber slices and boil for 10 minutes. Leave to stand for 12 hours. Boil for 15 minutes, remove ginger, pour into hot jars and cover.

Grapefruit Conserve

6 medium grapefruit
2 lb cooking apples
1 pint orange juice
2 lb sugar

Peel the grapefruit and remove all the pith. Take out the segments of fruit from their skin. Peel, core and slice the apples, and just cover with water. Simmer until the juice runs. Strain the juice, of which 1 pint is needed. If there is not enough, use more apples to make enough. Mix the apple and orange juices and sugar, and stir over low heat until the sugar has dissolved. Bring to a slow boil, and boil for 10 minutes. Add the grapefruit pieces and boil slowly for 20 minutes. Pour into hot jars and cover.

Greengages in Syrup

4 lb greengages
4 lb sugar
1 pint water

Use firm, under-ripe fruit. Make a syrup with the sugar and water. Cool the syrup, add the fruit, and heat just to boiling point. Leave to stand overnight and heat again. Leave overnight, then bring the mixture to the boil, without stirring, and pour into warm jars.

Green Tomato Preserve

3 lb green tomatoes
15 peach leaves
4 lb sugar
2 lemons
2 pieces root ginger
2 tablespoons brandy

Cover the tomatoes with water, add the peach leaves, and boil gently until the tomatoes are soft but not broken. Drain the water into another pan and stir in the sugar until dissolved. Boil to a syrup, strain and leave until cold. Peel the lemons thinly and put into a muslin bag with the crushed root ginger. Suspend the bag in the syrup. Put in the tomatoes and the juice of the lemons. Cook at a slow boil until the syrup will set. Stir in the brandy, pour into hot jars and cover.

Marrow Conserve

3 lb marrow flesh
2 lemons
$1\frac{1}{2}$ oz root ginger
3 lb sugar

Weigh the marrow when it has been peeled and seeded. Cut the flesh into cubes and steam until tender. Put into a bowl with the grated rind and juice of the lemon and the bruised root ginger in a muslin bag. Cover with sugar and leave for 24 hours. Put all ingredients into a pan, and heat slowly until the sugar has dissolved. Simmer for 1 hour until the marrow is transparent and the syrup is thick. Take out ginger, stir well, pour into hot jars and cover.

Orange Conserve

18 thin-skinned juicy oranges
Sugar

Prick 12 oranges well all over with a fork. Cover with water and leave to soak for three days, changing the water twice each day. Cover in fresh water, and simmer the oranges until tender. Drain and cover with cold water and leave for 24 hours. Cut each orange into eight sections and take out pips. Weigh the fruit and put into a pan with an equal weight of sugar. Add the juice of the remaining oranges, and stir until the sugar has dissolved. Simmer gently over low heat until the syrup reaches setting point. Pour into hot jars and cover. This is delicious eaten with cream.

Orange & Walnut Conserve

> 2 lb oranges
> 3 pints water
> 4 oz seedless raisins
> 2 lb sugar
> 2 oz walnut kernels

Grate the orange rinds finely. Peel the oranges and cup up the fruit, removing the pips. Simmer the orange flesh in the water for 30 minutes. Measure the pulp and make up to 2 pints if necessary with extra water. Add the rind, raisins and sugar. Heat gently, stirring well until the sugar has dissolved. Boil quickly for 20 minutes, and stir in roughly chopped walnuts. Bring to the boil, pour into hot jars and cover.

Pear Conserve

> 3 lb firm eating pears
> 1½ lemons
> 1¼ lb sugar

Peel and core the pears and cut the flesh into neat pieces. Peel the lemons thinly and squeeze out the juice. Boil the pear peel and cores and the lemon peel in ¼ pint water for 10 minutes, and strain. Put the liquid into a pan with the pears and lemon juice, and simmer until tender. Add the sugar and stir until dissolved. Bring to the boil, and boil to setting point. Pour into hot jars and cover.

Pear & Apple Conserve

$3\frac{1}{2}$ lb firm eating pears
$3\frac{1}{2}$ lb cooking apples
2 lemons
4 oz chopped mixed peel
5 lb sugar

Peel and core the pears and apples. Cut the flesh into small pieces. Add the grated rind and juice of the lemons, and the peel. Cover the pan and cook gently for 20 minutes. Leave overnight. Add the sugar, and heat gently, stirring until dissolved. Boil rapidly to setting point. Cool slightly, stir well, fill hot jars and cover.

Pear & Grape Conserve

$1\frac{1}{2}$ lb black grapes
$1\frac{1}{2}$ lb eating pears
1 inch cinnamon stick
3 lemons
Sugar

Simmer the grapes with the cinnamon stick in 4 tablespoons water for 10 minutes, and put through a sieve. Add water to make 1 pint of purée. Add the juice of the lemons. Peel and core the pears and cut them in thin slices. Simmer in the grape purée for 15 minutes. Measure the pears and liquid and add 12 oz sugar to each pint. Stir in sugar until dissolved, and boil rapidly to setting point. Pour into hot jars and cover.

Pear & Peach Conserve

2 lb eating pears
1½ lb peaches
3 lemons
3 lb sugar

Peel and core the pears and cut the flesh into cubes. Peel and slice the peaches. Put the pear pips and peach stones in a muslin bag and suspend in the cooking pan. Simmer pears and peaches in ¼ pint water until tender. Add the grated rind and juice of the lemons, together with the sugar. Stir until dissolved and boil rapidly to setting point. Pour into hot jars and cover.

Pear & Pineapple Conserve

2 lb ripe eating pears
8 fluid oz water
1 lb sugar
1 small fresh pineapple

Peel and core the pears, and cut them in thin slices. Put into a pan with water and sugar and bring slowly to the boil. Peel the pineapple and grate the flesh. Add pineapple to pears and simmer for 2 hours. Pour into hot jars and cover.

Pear Ginger (1)

4 lb pears
2 lb sugar
2 oz crystallised ginger
2 lemons

Do not peel the pears, but cut in quarters and remove the cores. Cut into small pieces. Add the sugar and the ginger cut into small pieces and leave to stand overnight. Cut the lemons into small pieces, removing the pips and add to the pears. Simmer for 3 hours, pour into hot jars and cover.

Pear Ginger (2)

 4 lb ripe eating pears
 4 lb sugar
 12 oz crystallised ginger
 2 lemons

Peel and core the pears and cut them into thin slices. Put into a pan with the sugar and finely chopped ginger. Boil slowly for 1 hour. Cut the lemons into small pieces and cover with water, include the pips and pith. Boil until the skins are soft. Strain the lemon liquid into the cooked pears. Boil until preserve is thick and clear. Pour into hot jars and cover.

Pear Ginger (3)

 2½ lb sugar
 2½ pints water
 3 lb hard winter pears
 1 lb crystallised ginger

Make a syrup with the sugar and water and boil for 1 minute. Peel, core and slice the pears, and slice the ginger. Put pears and ginger into syrup and boil slowly for 3 hours, without stirring. Pour into hot jars and cover.

Plum Conserve

 4 lb plums
 6 oz seedless raisins
 4 oz blanched almonds
 3 lb sugar

Cut the plums in half, and put the stones into a muslin bag. Suspend the bag in the cooking pan, and put in plums, raisins and a little water (unless the plums are very juicy). Simmer until the plums are soft. Add the sugar and stir until dissolved. Boil rapidly to setting point, stir in chopped almonds, put into hot jars and cover.

Plum Conserve with Rum

3 lb plums
8 tablespoons lemon juice
3½ lb sugar
4 tablespoons dark rum

Cut the plums into small pieces. Put into the pan with lemon juice and sugar. Bring to the boil, and boil hard for 3 minutes, stirring all the time. Add the rum. Leave to stand for 5 minutes, stirring often. Pour into hot jars and cover.

Plum Gumbo

5 lb plums
3 oranges
2 lb seedless raisins
5 lb sugar

Cut the plums in small pieces. Cut the oranges in thin slices, removing the pips. Chop the raisins finely. Put the fruit into a pan with the sugar and heat gently, stirring until the sugar has dissolved. Bring to boiling point and simmer until the consistency is like marmalade. Cool slightly, stir well, pour into warm jars and cover.

Prune Conserve

1 lb prunes
1½ pints water
1 teaspoon tartaric or citric acid
1 lb sugar

Put the prunes into the water and leave to soak for 24 hours. Put into a pan with the water and acid, cover and simmer until soft. Remove stones, and mash the fruit lightly as it cooks. Stir in sugar until it dissolves, then boil rapidly to setting point. Pour into hot jars and cover.

Pumpkin Preserve

1 medium pumpkin
4 lb sugar
8 oz butter
6 lemons

Peel the pumpkin and remove the seeds. Cut into pieces and steam for 30 minutes. Drain in a muslin bag for 24 hours. Weigh the remaining pulp (4 lb is needed for the remaining ingredients). Put into a pan with sugar, butter, the grated rind and juice of the lemons. Bring to the boil slowly, and then boil gently for 20 minutes. Pour into hot jars and cover. Because of the fat content, do not try to keep this preserve more than 2 months.

Raspberry Preserve

3 lb raspberries
3 lb sugar
1 oz butter

Warm a pan and rub it with the butter. Put in the raspberries and heat very slowly until the juice runs. Warm the sugar in the oven. Add the warm sugar to the raspberries and beat over a low heat for 30 minutes. Pour into hot jars and cover.

Rhubarb Preserve

$3\frac{1}{2}$ lb rhubarb
$3\frac{1}{2}$ lb sugar
1 lemon
2 oz blanched almonds

Peel the rhubarb and cut it into neat pieces. Put over a low heat until the juice runs. Add warm sugar, grated rind and juice of the lemon, and split almonds. Stir until sugar is dissolved, and boil for 45 minutes until thick and brown. Pour into hot jars and cover. This is a good way of using autumn rhubarb.

Rhubarb & Almond Preserve

2 lb rhubarb
2 lemons
$3\frac{1}{2}$ lb sugar
2 oz blanched almonds

Cut the rhubarb into short pieces. Put into a pan with the grated rind of the lemons and $\frac{1}{4}$ pint water. Simmer until the rhubarb is a pulp. Add the juice of the lemons, the sugar and the split almonds. Stir until the sugar has dissolved. Bring to the boil and boil to setting point. Pour into hot jars and cover.

Rhubarb & Angelica Preserve

4 lb rhubarb
3 lb sugar
$\frac{1}{2}$ teaspoon citric acid
8 oz crystallised angelica

Cut the rhubarb into short pieces and put in layers in a bowl with the sugar. Leave to stand overnight. Put into a pan, add the acid and bring to the boil, stirring well. Boil quickly to setting point. Take off the heat and add the angelica cut into small pieces. Stir well, pour into hot jars and cover.

Rhubarb & Ginger Preserve

$2\frac{1}{2}$ lb rhubarb
$2\frac{1}{2}$ lb sugar
1 oz root ginger
4 oz crystallised ginger

Cut the rhubarb into short pieces and put in layers in a bowl with the sugar. Leave overnight. Put into a pan with the bruised root ginger tied into a muslin bag. Bring to the boil, and boil hard for 15 minutes. Cut the crystallised ginger into small pieces, add to the mixture, and boil for 5 minutes. Remove the bag of root ginger, pour into hot jars and cover.

Rhubarb & Orange Preserve

> 4 lb rhubarb
> 4 lb sugar
> 6 oranges
> ½ teaspoon citric acid

Cut the rhubarb into short pieces. Grate the rind from the oranges and squeeze out the juice. Put the rhubarb, orange rind and juice into a bowl and leave for 12 hours. Put into a pan with the sugar and add the acid. Bring to the boil, stirring well until the sugar has dissolved. Boil hard to setting point, pour into hot jars and cover.

Strawberries in Syrup

> Strawberries
> Sugar

Clean and hull the strawberries and put into a dish with an equal weight of sugar, arranged in layers. Leave for 24 hours. Boil for 5 minutes. Leave for 24 hours, then boil for 7 minutes. Put into hot jars and cover.

Sunshine Strawberries

> Strawberries
> Sugar

Use perfectly shaped strawberries for this. Put them into a pan with an equal weight of sugar, arranged in layers. Leave to stand for 30 minutes, then bring to boiling point and cook for 20 minutes. Arrange on plates, cover with glass, and put in the sun for several days until the syrup is thick, stirring several times each day. Pour into jars and cover.

Wild Strawberries in Syrup

2 lb wild (or Alpine) strawberries
12 oz sugar

Put strawberries into a bowl and sprinkle with sugar. Leave to stand overnight. Drain off the syrup the next day, bring to the boil, and boil for 3 minutes. Add the strawberries and simmer 30 minutes. Pour into small hot jars and cover. The strawberries will be floating in syrup, and are delicious with ice cream.

CHAPTER TEN
Mincemeats

Mincemeat was originally made with minced meat, mixed with dried fruit and highly spiced and the original mince pie was made in the shape of a crib to celebrate Christmas. Today's round mince pie is filled with a mixture of beef suet (a reminder of the traditional minced meat), apples, dried fruit and spice, moistened with spirits which improve both flavour and keeping quality. Mincemeat is better for maturing a week or two before using, and will remain fresh and juicy for several weeks.

A mixture of minced, chopped and whole fruit gives the best texture and appearance. Mincemeat should be packed into clean, dry, cold jars, and can be covered like jam. A thicker cover of brown paper or greaseproof paper, a plastic top, or a preserving jar cover will prevent evaporation and drying out. If the mixture does become a little dry, extra spirits may be stirred in before the mincemeat is used.

Basic Mincemeat (1)

> 2 lb cooking apples
> 12 oz grated beef suet
> 8 oz raisins
> 8 oz sultanas
> 1 lb currants
> 8 oz chopped mixed peel
> 1 lemon
> 1 tablespoon powdered cinnamon
> 1½ lb sugar
> 2 teaspoons salt
> 1 gill brandy
> 1 gill sherry

Put the apples through the mincer with the suet, dried fruit, and peel. Add the juice and grated rind of the lemon. Mix well with remaining ingredients, and cover with a cloth. Leave in a cold place for 12 hours. Stir well and leave for another 12 hours. Pack into clean jars and cover tightly. This mincemeat improves with keeping about six weeks.

Basic Mincemeat (2)

8 oz cooking apples
8 oz grated beef suet
8 oz raisins
8 oz currants
8 oz sultanas
4 oz chopped mixed peel
1 lemon
4 oz moist brown sugar
1 oz chopped nuts
2 tablespoons brandy *or* sherry

Put apples, suet, dried fruit and peel through the mincer. Mix together with the grated rind and juice of the lemon, sugar, nuts, brandy or sherry. Pack into clean jars and cover at once.

One-week Mincemeat

8 oz cooking apples
8 oz currants
8 oz raisins
4 oz chopped mixed peel
4 oz Demerara sugar
8 oz white grapes
Grated rind
Grated rind of 1 orange
Grated rind of 1 lemon
1 tablespoon lemon juice
1 teaspoon mixed spice
Pinch of salt

This mincemeat contains no suet and will only keep for a week in a cool place, but it is very useful for making quickly when supplies run low. Peel and core the apples and cut into small pieces. Mix with the raisins, currants, peel and sugar. Add peeled and stoned grapes which have been roughly chopped. Mix with orange and lemon rinds and juice, cinnamon and salt. Pot and cover, and store in a cold place.

Cider Mincemeat

12 oz cooking apples
12 oz stoned raisins
6 oz currants
6 oz soft brown sugar
2 teaspoons ground cinnamon
1 teaspoon ground cloves
1 teaspoon ground nutmeg
3 fluid oz cider
1 lemon
3 oz butter

This is another short-keeping mincemeat without suet. Chop the apples and raisins, and put into a pan with all the other ingredients, and the grated rind and juice of the lemon. Simmer for 30 minutes and moisten with a little brandy if necessary. Pack into jars and cover when cold.

Rum & Brown Sugar Mincemeat

1 lb cooking apples
1½ lb grated beef suet
1 lb currants
1 lb seeded raisins
1 lb sultanas
1 lb soft brown sugar (dark)
1 oz mixed spice
Grated rind of 2 lemons
Grated rind of 3 oranges
5 fluid oz rum
5 fluid oz brandy

Peel and core the apples and put through the mincer with the suet. Mix with the dried fruit, sugar, spice, rind of lemons and oranges, rum and brandy. Mix thoroughly. Pack into clean jars and cover at once. The large sticky raisins are best for this. They should be stoned, and roughly chopped.

Cooked Mincemeat

$\frac{3}{4}$ pint apple juice (see method)
1 lb seedless raisins
1 lb currants
1 lb grated beef suet
$1\frac{1}{2}$ lb soft brown sugar
6 lb cooking apples
1 lb chopped mixed peel
$\frac{1}{2}$ teaspoon ground mace
$1\frac{1}{2}$ teaspoons cinnamon
3 fluid oz brandy

Make the apple juice by mincing a large quantity of apples, and squeezing them in butter muslin to get a clear juice. In a large pan, put the juice and bring it rapidly to the boil. Add dried fruit, suet, brown sugar, chopped apples, peel and spices. Simmer slowly for 1 hour. Stir in the brandy. Put into sterilised preserving jars. This mincemeat will keep for 1 year.

Pear & Apricot Mincemeat

$1\frac{1}{2}$ lb firm eating pears
1 lb currants
1 lb raisins
8 oz glacé apricots
12 oz chopped mixed peel
12 oz grated beef suet
1 lb soft brown sugar
1 tablespoon mixed spice

1 tablespoon cinnamon
1 tablespoon ground ginger
1 tablespoon ground cloves
3 tablespoons brandy

This is a very spicy mixture. If it is a bit dry, mix with a
little sherry. Peel, core and chop the pears and mix
with the dried fruit, chopped apricots, peel, suet, sugar,
spices and brandy. Mix well and put into clean jars.
Cover at once.

Almond Mincemeat

1½ lb cooking apples
1 lb grated beef suet
1 lb sultanas
1 lb currants
1 lb raisins
1 lb Demerara sugar
1 lb chopped mixed peel
6 oz blanched almonds
2 lemons
1 teaspoon ground nutmeg
½ teaspoon ground cinnamon
½ teaspoon ground allspice
½ teaspoon salt
¼ pint brandy or rum

Peel and core the apples, and grate into a bowl. Mince
the raisins. Shred the almonds. Mix together apples,
suet, dried fruit, sugar, peel and almonds, the grated
rind and juice of the lemon, spices, salt, and brandy or
rum. When thoroughly blended, pack into clean dry
jars and cover. Leave in a dry cool place for 3 weeks
before using.

Lemon Mincemeat

3 large lemons
3 large cooking apples
1 lb stoned raisins
8 oz currants
1 lb grated beef suet
4 oz chopped mixed peel
2 tablespoons bitter orange marmalade
5 fluid oz brandy

Grate the lemon rinds and squeeze out the juice. Remove the pith from the lemon peel, and then boil the peel until very tender. Put through the mincer. Bake the apples, and remove the skin. Mash the apple pulp and mix with the lemon peel, dried fruit, suet, sugar, peel, marmalade and brandy. Put into jars and cover tightly and keep for 2 weeks before using.

Glacé Fruit Mincemeat

8 oz chopped mixed peel
2 cooking apples
1 lb grated beef suet
4 oz blanched almonds
1 lb seedless raisins
1 lb currants
1 lb sultanas
12 oz soft brown sugar
4 oz glacé cherries
2 oz crystallised ginger
1 oz glacé pineapple
½ teaspoon salt
½ teaspoon ground nutmeg
½ teaspoon mixed spice
1 orange
1 lemon
¼ pint brandy or light rum

Peel and core the apples. Put peel, apples, suet and raisins through the coarse blade of the mincer. Shred the almonds, and chop finely the cherries, ginger and pineapple. Grate the rind from the orange and lemon, and squeeze out the juice. Mix all the ingredients thoroughly and pack into clean dry jars. Cover tightly and store in a cool place for 2 weeks before using.

CHAPTER ELEVEN
Jams made with Dried Fruit

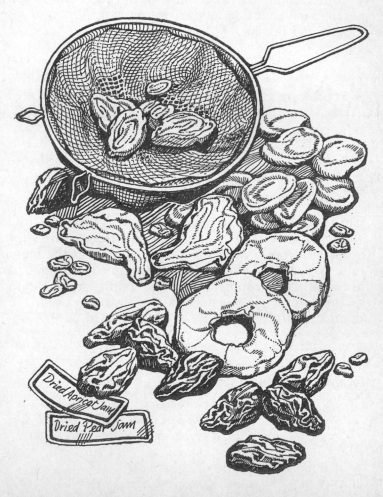

Dried Apricot Jam

Dried Pear Jam

Jam can be usefully made with dried fruit when supplies of fresh fruit are low. They are particularly good made in the late autumn when shop supplies of dried fruit are fresh and juicy. For economy, bulk fruit such as apples and rhubarb can be added to the dried fruits. Usually the dried fruit must be soaked for about 24 hours before the jam is made, and lemon juice, tartaric or citric acid aid setting and sharpen the flavour. Some of these jams are rather thick and particularly suitable for tart fillings and for pastry or shortbread fingers.

Apricot or Peach Jam

1 lb dried apricots or peaches
3 pints water
Juice of 1 lemon *or* 1 teaspoon
  citric or tartaric acid
3 lb sugar
3 oz blanched almonds (optional)

Cut up the apricots or peaches and leave to soak in the water for at least 24 hours. Put the water and fruit into a pan and boil gently for 30 minutes. Add the lemon juice or acid and the sugar and stir until the sugar has dissolved. Boil rapidly to setting point, stirring often as the jam tends to stick. If almonds are used, they should be added with the sugar. Pot and cover.

Apricot & Date Jam

1 lb dried apricots
1½ lb chopped dates
2 pints water
8 oz sugar
Juice of 1 lemon
2 oz chopped almonds

Soak the apricots overnight in half the water. Add the dates and remaining water and cook over low heat until the apricots are soft. Add the sugar and lemon juice, and stir until the sugar has dissolved. Continue cooking slowly, stirring well, until the jam is thick. Stir in nuts, and cook for 5 minutes. Pour into hot jars and cover at once. This makes an excellent filling for tarts or shortbread biscuits.

Apricot & Lemon Jam

    1 lb lemons
    1 lb dried apricots
    3 pints water
    3 lb sugar

Slice the lemons thinly and cut the slices in quarters. Put the pips into a muslin bag. Put lemons into a bowl with the apricots and water and leave to stand overnight. Put the mixture into a pan, and suspend the pips into the liquid. Simmer until lemon peel is soft. Add sugar and stir until dissolved. Boil rapidly to setting point, pot and cover. A mixture of oranges and lemons may be used instead of only lemons.

Apricot & Pear Jam

    1 lb dried apricots
    1 pint water
    3 lb pears
    Juice of 2 lemons
    $3\frac{1}{2}$ lb sugar

Soak the apricots overnight in the water. Put into a pan with the pears which have been peeled, cored and chopped. Add the lemon juice, and simmer for 10 minutes. Stir in the sugar until dissolved and boil quickly to setting point. Pot and cover. This is particularly delicious if 3 tablespoons liqueur (Apricot

Brandy, Grand Marnier or Curaçao) are stirred in just before potting.

Apricot & Pineapple Jam

> 1 medium-sized fresh pineapple
> 1 lb dried apricots
> 3 lemons
> 4 lb sugar

Peel the pineapple and cut the flesh into cubes. Save the juice and add water to make up 3 pints. Put water and juice into a bowl with the apricots and leave to soak overnight. Put apricots and liquid into a pan with the grated rind and juice of the lemons. Simmer until tender. Crush the pineapple (this can easily be done in a blender), and add to the mixture with the sugar. Stir until the sugar has dissolved, bring to the boil, and boil for 15 minutes. Pot and cover.

Date Jam

> $1\frac{1}{2}$ lb stoned dates
> $\frac{3}{4}$ pint water
> $\frac{3}{4}$ lb sugar
> 1 small lemon
> Pinch of ground cinnamon
> Pinch of ground nutmeg
> 1 oz fresh butter

Cut up the dates and put into pan with water. Bring to the boil slowly, and simmer for 10 minutes. Add the sugar, grated rind and juice of the lemon, spices and butter. Simmer and stir until the mixture is thick and smooth. Pour into small warm jars and cover. This is very good as a filling for biscuits or pastry fingers.

Date & Apple Jam

2½ lb cooking apples
2 lb sugar
Juice of 2 lemons
12 oz dessert dates

Peel and core the apples and cut into thin slices. Cover with the sugar and lemon juice and leave for 6 hours. Put into pan and stir over low heat until the sugar has dissolved. Remove stones from the dates and cut the fruit into two or three pieces. Add to the apples and simmer until jam reaches setting point. Pot and cover.

Fig & Apple Jam

2 lb dried figs
6 lb cooking apples
3 lemons
½ teaspoon ground cinnamon
½ teaspoon ground cloves
½ teaspoon nutmeg
3 pints water
5 lb sugar

Remove stalks from the figs. Peel and core the apples. Put figs and apples through the coarse blade of a mincer, or chop them finely. Put into pan with grated rind and juice of the lemons, spices and water. Simmer until the fruit is soft. Add the sugar and stir until dissolved. Bring to the boil and boil for 5 minutes. Pot and cover.

Fig & Rhubarb Jam

8 oz dried figs
2 lb rhubarb
2 lb sugar
Juice of 1 lemon

Cut up the figs and rhubarb finely. Mix with the sugar and lemon juice and leave to stand for 24 hours. Bring to the boil, stirring well. Boil rapidly to setting point. Leave to cool for 30 minutes, stir well, pot and cover.

Fruit Salad Jam

> 1 lb dried fruit salad (apples,
>   pears, apricots, prunes)
> 3 pints water
> Juice of 1 lemon
> 3 lb sugar

Cut up the fruit and leave to soak in the water for 24 hours. Put the water and fruit into a pan and boil gently for 30 minutes. Add the lemon juice and the sugar and stir until the sugar has dissolved. Boil rapidly to setting point, stirring well. Pot and cover. This makes a good and unusual breakfast jam, or tart filling.

Prune Jam

> 2 lb prunes
> 2½ pints water
> 2 lemons
> 1¾ lb sugar

Soak prunes overnight in water. Boil the prunes in the water for 30 minutes. Lift out prunes and remove stones. Add the grated rind and juice of the lemons to the cooking water, together with the sugar. Stir until the sugar has dissolved, then bring to the boil and boil for 5 minutes. Add the prunes and boil until jam is at setting point. Put into clean dry pots, and cover. Some of the kernels from the stones may be peeled and added.

Tipsy Apricots

8 oz dried apricots
1 pint boiling water
1 lb granulated sugar
¼ pint cold water
12 tablespoons gin or brandy

Put the apricots into a bowl, pour on boiling water, and leave to soak overnight. Drain the fruit, and chop roughly. Dissolve the sugar in the cold water over a gentle heat. Add the apricots and bring to the boil. Simmer for 15 minutes. Leave for 2 hours until cold. Stir in gin or brandy, and store in screw-top jars. This makes a delicious filling for cakes or pastry cases, or can be used as a sauce for ices or puddings.

Rum Raisins

8 oz caster sugar
¼ pint water
8 oz seedless raisins
6 tablespoons rum

Stir sugar into water and bring gently to the boil, stirring all the time. Add raisins and simmer for 15 minutes. Cool for 2 hours and stir in rum. Store in screw-top jars. This makes a very good sauce for ices, and hot or cold puddings.

CHAPTER TWELVE
Jams made with Canned and Frozen Fruit

Delicious jams can be made with canned and frozen fruit. This means that fruit such as pineapple and blueberries can be used cheaply, and at any time of the year. Canned fruit pulps are also available, specially prepared for jam-making, and these are useful for making a fresh supply of out-of-season jam such as apricot or raspberry. Full directions for using this pulp are on each can.

Fruit for jam-making may be frozen during the summer, to be converted at a later date. The fruit should be prepared (e.g. strawberries hulled or cherries pipped) and frozen in suitable quantities without sugar. Two pound bags are useful for jam-making purposes. A certain amount of pectin (setting agent) is lost in freezing, and with poor-setting fruit such as strawberries, about 10% extra frozen fruit will be needed, so it is wise to freeze an extra bag of fruit to deal with this increase.

When the frozen fruit is needed, it should be placed in the jam pan with about $\frac{1}{2}$ pint water, and heated very gently until the juices begin to run. The procedure is then the same as for jam-making with fresh fruit, using the same amounts of sugar and any necessary acid.

Fruit may be frozen with 20% of its weight in sugar, which helps to preserve the colour. If this method is followed, a note should be made of the added weight of sugar, so that it can be deducted from the quantity to be used for jam-making.

Another way of using frozen fruit to make jam which can be stored in the freezer is given in detail in Chapter Thirteen FREEZER JAMS.

Blueberry Jam (Frozen Fruit)

2 lb frozen blueberries
2 lb sugar

Put frozen blueberries into preserving pan with $\frac{1}{2}$ pint water. Heat gently until the juices start to run. Stir in the sugar until dissolved and boil steadily for 20 minutes until set. Pour into hot sterilised jars and cover. This jam should not be boiled quickly or the blueberries will lose their shape. The jam sets quickly and firmly.

Fig & Apple Jam (Canned Fruit)

> 4 lb cooking apples
> 30 oz canned figs in syrup
> 1 pint water
> 6 lb sugar

Peel and core the apples and chop into pieces. Chop the figs and add to the apples with the syrup from the can and the water. Simmer for 1 hour to setting point. Pour into hot sterilised jars and cover.

Pear & Pineapple Conserve (Canned Fruit)

> 6 lb pears
> 30 oz canned pineapple in syrup
> 2 oranges
> Sugar
> $\frac{1}{2}$ pint maraschino cherries in syrup

This can be made with large broken pieces of pineapple. It is a delicious conserve to use as a tart filling, as a sauce for ice cream, or as a rich dessert with cream.

Wipe the pears and remove stems and cores, but do not peel. Cut into small pieces. Add pineapple and juice, together with juice and grated rind of oranges. Weigh the mixture and add three-quarters weight in sugar. Leave to stand overnight. Simmer until thick and syrupy, and add the cherries cut in half, together with their liquid. Stir well and fill small jars.

Pineapple & Apricot Jam (Canned Fruit)

1 lb dried apricots
3½ pints water
13 oz canned pineapple tidbits
4 lb sugar

Soak the apricots in the water overnight. Put into preserving pan and add sugar, pineapple and juice from the can. Bring very slowly to the boil, stirring occasionally. When the sugar has dissolved, boil rapidly for 1 hour to setting point. Pour into hot sterilised jars and cover.

Pineapple & Orange Jam (Canned Fruit)

2 oranges
1 pint water
30 oz canned pineapple in syrup
Sugar

Soak the oranges in water overnight, then boil them until soft. Remove from the water and cut into small pieces, removing pips. Add 1 lb sugar to each pound of fruit. Heat gently together, stirring until the sugar has dissolved. Boil about 30 minutes to setting point. Pour into hot sterilised jars and cover.

CHAPTER THIRTEEN
Freezer Jams

Uncooked jams which can be stored in the freezer for six months save a certain amount of preparation time and work. These jams are brightly coloured and have the delicious smell of fresh fruit. Since the fruit is ripe and uncooked, it retains the maximum fresh fruit flavour.

Ingredients for these jams must be measured carefully, and instructions followed closely. The jams contain a high proportion of sugar, and the yield for each lb of fruit is high. The jams are mixed and then left to set before freezing. After the first five hours at room temperature, the jams should be put into a refrigerator to finish setting before storage in the freezer. They are best packed in small quantities in rigid containers with tight-fitting lids, allowing $\frac{1}{2}$ in. headspace.

Freezer jam should be stored at 0°F or lower, and will keep for six months. Sometimes a white mouldlike formation is noticeable when the jams are removed from the freezer, but this is not harmful and will melt quickly at room temperature. Jams should be thawed for 1 hour before service. After opening, they should be stored in the refrigerator and used up quickly. If these uncooked jams are stiff, or if 'weeping' has occurred, they should be lightly stirred to soften and blend before serving.

These jams may be made from fresh or frozen fruit, and individual methods are given below.

Fresh Apricot or Peach Jam

> $1\frac{1}{2}$ lb ripe fresh apricots or peaches
> 2 lb caster sugar
> 4 fluid oz liquid pectin
> 1 teaspoon powdered citric acid

Skin the apricots or peaches and remove the stones. Mash the fruit and stir in citric acid and sugar. Leave for 20 minutes, stirring occasionally, then add pectin and stir for 3 minutes. Put into small containers, cover and seal. Leave for 5 hours at room temperature, then put into refrigerator until jelled. This may take 24–48 hours. Store in freezer. Thaw for 1 hour at room temperature before serving.

Fresh Blackberry Jam

1½ lb blackberries
2¾ lb caster sugar
4 fluid oz liquid pectin

Small hard wild blackberries are difficult to mash without liquid and may be 'pippy', so this jam is better made with large cultivated blackberries. Mash the blackberries and stir in sugar. Leave for 20 minutes, stirring occasionally, then add pectin and stir for 3 minutes. Put into small containers, cover and seal. Leave for 5 hours at room temperature, then put into refrigerator until jelled. This may take 24–48 hours. Store in freezer. Thaw for 1 hour at room temperature before serving.

Fresh Cherry Jam

1½ lb Morello cherries
2 lb caster sugar
4 fluid oz liquid pectin

Remove stones from cherries and put through coarse blade of a mincer. Stir with sugar and leave for 20 minutes, stirring occasionally. Add pectin and stir for 3 minutes. Put into small containers, cover and seal. Leave for 5 hours at room temperature, then put into refrigerator until jelled. This may take 24–48 hours. Store in freezer. Thaw for 1 hour at room temperature before serving.

Fresh Plum Jam

1½ lb Victoria plums
2 lb caster sugar
2 teaspoons lemon juice
4 fluid oz liquid pectin

Remove stones from plums and stir in sugar and lemon juice. Leave for 20 minutes, stirring occasionally. Add pectin and stir for 3 minutes. Put into small containers, cover and seal. Leave for 5 hours at room temperature, then put into refrigerator until jelled. This may take 24–48 hours. Store in freezer. Thaw for 1 hour at room temperature before serving.

Fresh Raspberry Jam

1½ lb raspberries
3 lb caster sugar
4 fluid oz liquid pectin

Mash or sieve the raspberries and stir with the sugar. Leave for 20 minutes, stirring occasionally, then add pectin and stir for 3 minutes. Put into small containers, cover and seal. Leave for 5 hours at room temperature, then put into refrigerator until jelled. This may take 24–48 hours. Store in freezer. Thaw for 1 hour at room temperature before serving.

Fresh Strawberry Jam

1½ lb strawberries
2 lb caster sugar
4 fluid oz liquid pectin

Mash or sieve the strawberries and stir with the sugar. Leave for 20 minutes, stirring occasionally, then add pectin and stir for 3 minutes. Put into small containers, cover and seal. Leave for 5 hours at room temperature, then put into refrigerator until jelled. This may take 24–48 hours. Store in freezer. Thaw for 1 hour at room temperature before serving.

Frozen Cherry Jam

1¾ lb cherries frozen in sugar
1½ lb caster sugar
1 teaspoon lemon juice
4 fluid oz liquid pectin

Thaw cherries and put through coarse blade of a mincer. Add lemon juice and sugar and stir well. Leave to stand for 20 minutes, stirring occasionally. Stir in pectin for 3 minutes. Put into small containers, cover and seal, and leave at room temperature for 24 hours. Store in freezer. Thaw for 1 hour at room temperature before serving.

Frozen Peach Jam

1¼ lb peaches frozen in sugar
1½ lb caster sugar
1½ tablespoons lemon juice
4 fluid oz liquid pectin

Thaw fruit and mash with sugar and lemon juice. Leave to stand for 20 minutes, stirring occasionally. Stir in pectin for 3 minutes. Put into small containers, cover and seal, and leave at room temperature for 24 hours. Store in freezer. Thaw for 1 hour at room temperature before serving.

Frozen Raspberry Jam

1¾ lb raspberries frozen in sugar
2 lb caster sugar
4 fluid oz liquid pectin

Thaw raspberries and mash well. Stir in sugar and leave to stand for 20 minutes, stirring occasionally. Stir in pectin for 3 minutes. Put into small containers, cover and seal, and leave at room temperature for 24 hours. Store in freezer. Thaw for 1 hour at room temperature before serving.

Frozen Strawberry Jam

> 1¼ lb strawberries frozen in sugar
> 1½ lb caster sugar
> 4 fluid oz liquid pectin

Thaw strawberries and mash well. Stir in sugar and leave to stand for 20 minutes, stirring occasionally. Stir in pectin for 3 minutes. Put into small containers, cover and seal, and leave at room temperature for 24 hours. Store in freezer. Thaw for 1 hour at room temperature before serving.

CHAPTER FOURTEEN
Flower Jams and Jellies

Flower jams and jellies were made by our ancestors, not only for their delicious flavour but also for their therapeutic qualities, since they were reputed to be soothing. Such disorders as melancholy and giddiness were supposed to be cured by these little concoctions. Rose and violet jams were particularly associated with the Near East in the seventeenth century, and one or two of the recipes are included in this chapter.

These jams and jellies are perhaps no more than an interesting curiosity now, but they can be delicious eaten on small biscuits or thin bread and butter, or taken as a sweetmeat with a spoon. Such confections used to be set in pretty little china dishes ready for the tea table.

Those who do not wish to make even small quantities of these unusual jams might however enjoy delicate flower flavours in fruit jellies. Gooseberry jelly cooked with elderflowers (tied in a muslin bag) has a delicate muscat flavour. Apple or gooseberry jelly is particularly delicious if flavoured with a leaf of rose geranium, lemon geranium or peppermint geranium. The flavour is best if one or two leaves are cooked with the fruit, and another leaf added to the juice being boiled with sugar.

Conserve of Flowers

    4 lb cooking apples
    2 pints water
    8 oz flower petals (carnations, jasmine,
        primroses, violets, roses)
    Sugar

Choose the flowers according to the season of the year. Cut the fruit in pieces and put into preserving pan with water and flower petals. Simmer until the fruit is pulpy, and strain through a jelly bag. Measure the juice and allow 1 lb sugar to each pint of juice. Stir in the sugar until dissolved, and boil rapidly to setting point.

Cowslip Cheese

1½ lb cowslip flowers
2½ pints boiling water
Sugar

This deep yellow cheese, which is a kind of thick paste, was supposed to be a cure for giddiness.

Put the cowslip flowers into a bowl and pour over boiling water. Leave for 24 hours to infuse. Strain the liquid and measure. Allow 1 lb sugar to each pint of liquid. Stir sugar into the liquid over low heat until dissolved, and then boil to a thick paste. Pour into very small, straight-sided pots.

Marigold Conserve

5 oz marigold petals
1 lb sugar
Lemon juice

Pound the petals (using a pestle and mortar, or a blender on slow speed). Make them very small, adding a little lemon juice to aid the process if necessary. Gradually work in the sugar until it is thoroughly absorbed. Put into small jars and cover. This was originally valued as a cure for melancholy.

Rose Petal Conserve (1)

1 lb sugar
1 tablespoon water
1 lb dark red rose petals
1 dessertspoon orange flower or rose-water

Boil the sugar and water slowly to make a syrup. Wash and dry flower petals and stir into the syrup with the orange flower or rose-water. Simmer to a thick syrup and pour into small jars. The mixture will not set.

Rose Petal Conserve (2)

> 1 lb dark red rose petals
> 1 lb sugar
> ¼ pint rose-water
> 1 tablespoon orange flower water

Spread petals to dry in a light draught but away from direct sunlight. Put into a strainer and dip in boiling water for a second, then drain and dry petals. Heat sugar, rose-water and orange flower water gently to make a light syrup. Put in the rose petals and simmer for 45 minutes, stirring occasionally, until the mixture is soft and thick. Pour into small jars.

Rose Petal Jelly

> **Apple juice (see method)**
> **Rose petals**
> **Sugar**

Before beginning, petals from scented roses should be lightly dried. Those from old red roses such as *Etoile d'Hollande* are best, but other strongly scented red roses are good. The white 'heels' of the petals should be cut away, and the petals should be dried in a slight draught, away from direct sunshine. Cut up some unpeeled cooking apples in small pieces and cover with cold water. Simmer to a pulp, and strain through a jelly bag overnight. Allow 1 lb sugar to 1 pint liquid, and stir over low heat until the sugar has dissolved. Add as many dried rose petals as the liquid will hold, and boil until the jelly sets on a cold plate. Strain and pour into warm jars. The jelly has the colour and scent of roses.

Alternative method

Strongly-perfumed rose petals may be pounded with caster sugar and then cooked slowly in very little water in a covered pan until colour and scent are released.

The liquid should then be strained and added to the apple juice which is then boiled with sugar to setting point. This, of course, gives a clear jelly.

Rose Petal Jam

> 1 lb dark red rose petals
> 1½ lb sugar
> ½ pint water
> Juice of ½ lemon

Snip the white bases from the petals and cut the petals into pieces which are not too small. Put into a basin with half the sugar, cover and leave to stand for 48 hours. Dissolve the remaining sugar in the water and lemon juice, then stir in the rose petals and bring to the boil. Simmer for 20 minutes until the jam thickens. Pour into small jars and cover.

Rose Petal & Rhubarb Jam

> 4 oz dark red rose petals
> 1 lb rhubarb
> Juice of 1 lemon
> 1 lb sugar

Prepare the rhubarb and leave it to stand overnight with the lemon juice and sugar. Cut the rose petals in pieces and add to the mixture. Bring to the boil, and boil to setting point. Pour into small hot jars and cover.

Turkish Rose Petal Jam

> 1 lb dark red rose petals
> 2½ lb caster sugar

Trim the white bases of the rose petals and discard them. Put the petals into a bowl with the sugar and work with a wooden spoon until the petals have been pulped. Fill small glass jars and leave in strong sun-shine for a day. Cover the jars, and repeat the process next day. Cover the jars each night, and expose them to the sun each day for a month, until the top of the jam is crystallised. Cover and store in a cool place.

Violet Jam

$\frac{1}{2}$ **lb violet flowers**
1 pint boiling water
1$\frac{1}{2}$ lb sugar

Put three-quarters of the flowers into a bowl and cover with boiling water. Cover and leave for 15 hours. Strain the liquid through a jelly bag. Add the sugar and stir until dissolved. Bring to the boil, add the remaining flowers, and boil to setting point. Pour into small jars and cover.

CHAPTER FIFTEEN
Old-fashioned Fruits

In old gardens and orchards, the four 'old-fashioned' fruits may still be found: figs, medlars, mulberries and quinces. Many trees have been destroyed because the owners lacked knowledge of the ways in which their fruit might be used. The fruit of all four trees is particularly delicious in jams and jellies, and new trees are worth planting. Quinces and figs appear in many nurserymen's catalogues, but mulberries and medlars are harder to find.

Medlars are shaped like large round rose-hips, the colour of unripe russet apples and very hard. They should be gathered and kept for some weeks until soft or 'bletted'. The soft brown flesh may be mashed with thick cream and brown sugar, or they can be baked like apples with butter and cloves. Jelly made from medlars is dark red, and very good as a spread, or served with game.

Mulberries were planted so that the leaves could be used as food for silkworms. The fruits are like large crimson loganberries and fall when ripe. Hay, straw or paper should be spread beneath the tree during the season to catch the ripe fruit. Mulberry juice stains very badly indeed. The fruit can be used in every recipe for raspberries or loganberries and is good eaten fresh with sugar and cream, or made into a pie, or cooked in the oven with sugar to eat with milk pudding or with cream.

Quinces are hard, yellow and pear-shaped when ripe. The raw flesh is bitter and unattractive, but when cooked it becomes a rich pink-red and releases a beautiful fragrance and flavour. The flavour blends well with apples, pears, oranges, lemons and cloves, and the fruit may be used for a number of preserves.

Fig Jam

1 lb fresh figs
8 oz apples
Juice of 3 lemons
Grated rind of 1 lemon
1 lb sugar

Wash the figs, peel them, and blanch in boiling water for 1 minute. Drain the figs, rinse them in cold water, and cut in thin slices. Peel and slice the apples. Put figs and apples into the pan with lemon juice and rind. Cover and cook slowly until the fruit is tender. Add the sugar and stir until dissolved. Boil rapidly for 15 minutes, pour into hot jars and cover. The jam may also be flavoured with a small piece of cinnamon stick, root ginger, and a couple of cloves tied in muslin and removed before the jam is potted.

Medlar Cheese

2 lb medlars
Juice of 2 lemons
$\frac{1}{2}$ pint water
Sugar
1 teaspoon mixed spice

Cut the medlars into quarters. Put into a pan with the lemon juice and water, and simmer until the fruit is soft. Sieve and weigh the pulp. Allow 12 oz sugar to each lb pulp. Stir in sugar until it has dissolved and add the spice. Bring to the boil and boil hard for 5 minutes, stirring all the time. Pour into hot jars and cover.

Medlar Jam

4 lb very ripe medlars
Sugar
Vanilla pod

Scrape the pulp from very ripe medlars. Cook gently until very soft, adding very little water if necessary to prevent burning. Put through a sieve and weigh the pulp. Allow 12 oz sugar to each lb pulp. Stir until the sugar has dissolved. Put in the vanilla pod, and cook for 30 minutes, stirring all the time. Remove vanilla pod, pour into hot jars and cover.

Medlar Jelly

2 lb medlars
Sugar
1 lemon

Peel very ripe medlars, remove pips, and slice flesh into a pan with enough water to cover the fruit. Simmer with the cut-up lemon until soft. Strain the juice through a jelly bag. Allow 12 oz sugar to each pint of juice and stir until dissolved. Boil fast for 10 minutes until transparent. Skim well and cool slightly before pouring into jars. This can be eaten with bread and butter, or served with game.

Mulberry Jam

2 lb mulberries
1 lemon
1½ lb sugar

Rinse the mulberries lightly, and simmer until soft. Add the lemon rind and juice, and stir in the sugar until dissolved. Boil hard to setting point. Pour into hot jars and cover.

Mulberry & Apple Jam

> **3 lb mulberries**
> **1 lb apples**
> **1 pint water**
> **¼ oz citric acid**
> **3 lb sugar**

Rinse the mulberries. Peel and cut up the apples. Cook the fruit in water with the acid until pulpy. Stir in the sugar until dissolved and boil to setting point. Pour into hot jars and cover.

Mulberry Jelly

> **6 lb hard mulberries**
> **Sugar**

The mulberries should be fully-grown and red but not ripe. Simmer the fruit in 2 pints water for an hour. Add 2 pints water, and simmer for an hour, mashing the fruit with a spoon. Strain liquid through a jelly bag. Add 1 lb warm sugar to each pint of juice. Stir sugar until it dissolves and bring to boiling point. Skim well and continue boiling for 5 minutes. Pot and cover.

Mulberry Marmalade

> **4 lb ripe mulberries**
> **3 lb sugar**

Put 1 lb mulberries into a jar and stand it with a cover on in a low oven until the juice is extracted. The jar can be put in a pan of water on the stove instead of in the oven. Strain the juice and put into a pan with sugar. Bring to the boil and remove scum. Put in remaining mulberries and let them stand in the syrup until warmed through. Simmer very gently for 5 minutes, stirring all the time without breaking the fruit. Remove from the fire and leave to stand overnight. Boil gently to setting point, pot and cover.

Quince Butter

>   4 lb quinces
>   1 teaspoon citric or tartaric acid
>   Sugar

Peel the quinces and cut them up roughly. Almost cover with water and add the acid. Bring to the boil and simmer until the fruit is soft. Sieve and weigh the pulp. Allow 8 oz sugar to each lb pulp. Stir sugar until dissolved, bring to the boil, and boil for 45 minutes until creamy, stirring often. Pour into hot jars and cover.

Quince Cheese

>   3 lb quinces
>   1 orange
>   Sugar

Do not peel or core the quinces, but cut them up roughly. Chop the orange. Put into a pan with water just to cover and simmer until soft. Put through a sieve and weigh the pulp. Allow 1 lb sugar to each lb pulp. Stir sugar until dissolved and boil gently until almost solid, stirring often. Pour into hot jars and cover.

Quince Conserve

> $2\frac{1}{2}$ lb quinces
> $2\frac{3}{4}$ pints water
> $2\frac{3}{4}$ lb sugar

Peel and core the quinces and cut the flesh into small cubes. Put the cubes into 2 pints of water and bring to the boil. Add the sugar, remove from the heat and stir until the sugar is dissolved. Return to heat and cook gently until the fruit is soft but unbroken. Meanwhile put the cores and peel into the remaining water and cook until the pulp is reduced by half. Strain the liquid into the quinces. Boil hard to setting point. Cool a little and stir before putting into warm pots. This gives a clear red jelly with small cubes of quince.

Quince Honey

2 lb quinces
1 pint water
5 lb sugar

Peel the quinces. Grate the flesh into a bowl. Bring the water to the boil and stir in sugar. Gently dissolve the sugar over a low heat. Add the quinces and cook for 20 minutes. Pour into jars and cover. When the preserve is cold, it will be of the colour and consistency of honey.

Quince Jam

$2\frac{1}{2}$ lb quinces
$1\frac{1}{2}$ pints water
3 lb sugar

Peel, core and slice the quinces. Put into a pan with the water and simmer until the fruit is very soft. Add the sugar and stir until dissolved. Boil rapidly to setting point, pot and cover.

Quince & Apple Jam

4 lb quinces
4 lb apples
4 pints water
$1\frac{1}{2}$ lb sugar

Peel and slice the quinces and put into a pan with the water. Simmer gently until soft and strain the juice. Peel and slice the apples and cook in the quince juice for 45 minutes. Stir in the sugar until dissolved and boil for 20 minutes, stirring well. Remove scum, pour into pots and cover.

Quince & Cranberry Jam

$1\frac{1}{2}$ lb quinces
$\frac{3}{4}$ pint water
12 oz cranberries
$2\frac{1}{2}$ lb sugar

Peel and core the quinces and cut the flesh into small pieces. Cover with the water and simmer until soft. Put through a sieve. Add the pulp to the cranberries and simmer for 15 minutes. Stir in the sugar until dissolved. Bring to the boil and then simmer for 20 minutes. Pour into hot jars and cover.

Quince Jelly

4 lb quinces
6 pints water
Sugar

Wash the quinces and cut them up finely. Simmer in a pan with 4 pints water and the lid on for about 1 hour. Strain the liquid. Add the remaining water to the pulp and simmer for 30 minutes, then strain. Mix both strained liquids and allow 1 lb sugar to each pint. Bring the juice to the boil, stir in the sugar and bring back to the boil. Boil rapidly to setting point, skim, pot and cover.

Quince Marmalade

> 3 lb quinces
> 3 pints water
> 3 lb sugar
> 6 drops rose-water

Peel and core the quinces and cut the flesh into small pieces. Put into the pan with water and sugar and boil gently until soft. Put through a sieve and bring to the boil. Simmer until thick, remove from heat and stir in rose-water. Pour into small hot jars and cover.

Quince & Lemon Marmalade

> 1½ lb quinces
> 2 lemons
> 1 pint water
> 3 lb sugar

Peel and core the quinces, and cut the flesh into slices. Put into a pan with the juice of the lemons and the finely shredded lemon peel. Put the cores and peel of the quinces into a muslin bag and hang it in the saucepan. Simmer slowly for 45 minutes. Stir in warm sugar until dissolved, and boil rapidly to setting point. Remove the muslin bag. Leave marmalade to cool for a few minutes, stir well, and pour into pots.

Quince & Orange Marmalade

> 5 lb quinces
> 8 large sweet oranges
> 5 lb sugar

Cut the oranges into small pieces and shred the peel. Put the pips in a muslin bag. Cover the orange flesh, peel and pips with water and leave for 48 hours. Simmer in the same water with the pips until the peel is tender. Remove the pips. Stir in the sugar and leave to dissolve. Peel and core the quinces and cut the flesh into small pieces. Just cover with water and boil until pulpy. Strain the juice and add to the oranges. Boil hard for 30 minutes to setting point. Leave to cool for a few minutes, stir well and pour into pots.

Quince Preserve

Quinces
Sugar

Peel and core quinces and cut flesh into small cubes. Cover with just enough water to cook without burning. Simmer until fruit is soft but unbroken. Weigh and allow 1 lb sugar to each lb fruit. Stir in sugar and leave overnight. Bring to the boil and simmer for 20 minutes. Pour into hot jars and cover.

CHAPTER SIXTEEN
Jams from Abroad

British jams are noticeably different from those of other countries, perhaps because jam is associated with tea-time, a meal seldom eaten anywhere else in the world. The softly-textured jams with a good set, in which Britain specialises, are particularly good with bread and butter, toast, scones and all the other baked delicacies, and also with a variety of puddings unknown in Europe and America.

Foreign jams tend to be put up in small pots, suitable for use at breakfast time, and are made from a few choice fruit, rather than from glut quantities of apples and plums, for instance, as is common in this country. European jams are usually rather syrupy with whole fruit, and they are particularly useful for serving with pancakes, sweet omelettes and waffles. The jellies are richly flavoured, and very good for glazing cakes and flans.

The recipes in this chapter are for jams which have no popular British equivalent, and which are worth making in small quantities to provide variety in the store cupboard.

Angelica Jam

> 1 lb angelica stems
> 12 oz sugar
> 1 pint water

This jam is made from the stems of the angelica plant. Cut tender stems into strips and cook in boiling water until soft. Drain the stems, and then cover them in cold water and leave to soak for 12 hours. Make a syrup with the sugar and fresh water and cook until it begins to thicken. Add the angelica and cook to setting point. Pour into small jars and cover.

Chestnut Jam

1 lb chestnuts
12 oz sugar
1 pint water
1 vanilla pod

Boil and peel the chestnuts and sieve the kernels. Make a syrup with the sugar and water and vanilla pod (or use vanilla-flavoured sugar). When the sugar has dissolved, put in the sieved chestnuts and boil until fairly stiff. The jam should still be a little syrupy. Pour into small jars. This is very good served with thick cream and small sweet biscuits or sponge cakes.

Coconut Jam

1 fresh coconut
Sugar
1 vanilla pod

Break the coconut. Take out the white flesh and grate finely. Weigh the coconut flesh and weigh an equal quantity of sugar. Stir the sugar in very little water until dissolved. Bring to the boil, and add coconut and vanilla. Simmer for $1\frac{1}{2}$ hours, stirring often. Remove the vanilla pod, pour into small hot jars, and cover. This is a good filling for small sweet biscuits.

Grape Jam

2 lb grapes
1 lb sugar

Use grapes which are just ripe, but large and juicy. Remove the pips. Put grapes and sugar into a pan, bring slowly to the boil, and then cook slowly for 1 hour. Pour into small jars and cover.

Grapefruit Jam

> 4 large grapefruit
> 2 lb oranges
> 2 lb sugar

Peel the grapefruit and cut the flesh into small pieces, removing all pith. Squeeze the juice from the oranges, and heat this juice with the sugar, over a low heat. When the liquid boils, put in the grapefruit pieces. Cook for 20 minutes, stirring frequently. Put into hot jars and cover.

Green Fig Marmalade

> 1 lb ripe fresh figs
> 8 oz sugar
> $\frac{1}{2}$ pint water
> 1 cinnamon stick

The figs should be very juicy. Remove the stalks, but do not peel the fruit. Make a syrup with the sugar and water. Put in the figs and the cinnamon stick, and boil until the syrup becomes very thick. Remove the cinnamon stick, and pour into small jars.

Green Tomato Jam

> 3 lb green tomatoes
> $2\frac{1}{4}$ lb sugar
> 1 lemon

Cut green tomatoes in very thin slices and put in layers in a bowl with sugar. Leave for 24 hours. Put into a pan with the lemon cut in very small pieces. Simmer until the jam turns golden, pour into jars and cover. This is very good as a tart filling, topped with thick cream.

Eglantine (Wild Rose) Jam

Ripe wild rose hips
Red wine
Sugar

Remove the hairy pulp from the hips with a cocktail stick. Cover the pulp with red wine and leave for 6 weeks, adding a little more wine as it becomes absorbed so that the fruit is covered. Weigh the pulp and allow 12 oz sugar to each lb pulp. Simmer the mixture to setting point, then put through a sieve and pour into small jars.

Lemon Jam

Lemons
Sugar

Cut the lemons in thin slices without peeling them, and collect the pips in a muslin bag. Soak the lemons in water for 3 days, changing the water twice each day. Drain the slices and cook in lightly salted water until they are transparent. Drain well. Weigh the slices and allow 8 oz sugar to each lb lemons. Make a syrup with 8 oz sugar to 1 pint water. Boil for 10 minutes, then put in the lemon slices and the bag of pips. Boil for 30 minutes. Remove the pips, pour jam into hot jars and cover.

Melon Jam

4 lb ripe melon flesh
2 lb sugar
1 pint water
1 lemon

Cut the melon flesh into cubes. Make a syrup with the sugar and water and when the syrup is boiling, put in melon cubes. Cut the lemon in pieces, and suspend in the pan in a muslin bag. Cook gently until the jam is very thick. Remove lemon and pour jam into hot jars.

Melon & Raspberry Jam

$3\frac{1}{2}$ lb melon flesh
1 lb raspberries
4 lb sugar
1 lemon

Use a melon which is not too ripe. Cut the melon into cubes and put into a bowl in layers with the sugar, and the juice of the lemon. Leave for 12 hours. Bring to the boil and put in the raspberries. Cook gently for 30 minutes. Pour into hot jars and cover.

Melon Marmalade

4 lb ripe melon flesh
2 lb sugar

Cut the melon flesh into small cubes and arrange in layers with the sugar in a bowl. Leave for 24 hours. Put into a pan and cook slowly, stirring frequently to prevent burning. When the mixture is thick and golden, pour into jars.

Orange Jam

Oranges
Sugar

Cut the oranges into thin slices without peeling them, and collecting the pips in a muslin bag. Soak the slices in fresh water for 48 hours, changing the water twice daily. Drain the slices and cook them in slightly salted water until they are transparent. Drain well. Allow 8 oz sugar to each lb oranges. Make a syrup with 8 oz sugar to 1 pint water. Boil for 10 minutes, then put in the orange slices and the bag of pips. Boil for 30 minutes. Remove the pips, pour into hot jars and cover.

Pear Jam

4 lb pears
2 lb sugar
1 lemon

Peel and core the pears. Cut them in quarters and put into a bowl mixed with the sugar. Leave to stand for 24 hours. Boil quickly for 1 hour, stirring frequently, until the pears are cooked and at setting point (unripe pears will set more quickly). Grate the lemon rind and squeeze out the juice. Add the lemon rind halfway through cooking, and the juice about 5 minutes before the end of cooking time. Pour into hot jars and cover.

Walnut Jam

5 lb unripe walnuts
$3\frac{1}{2}$ lb sugar
$1\frac{1}{2}$ pints water

Use green walnuts in July. Peel the kernels to remove the bitter skin. Prick the walnuts all over with a needle and leave to soak for a week in water which is changed every day. Drain walnuts and boil for 10 minutes in water with a spoonful of vinegar. Drain thoroughly. Make a syrup with the sugar and water. Throw in walnuts and boil for 40 minutes. Pour into small jars.

Water Melon Jam

3 lb water melon flesh
2 lb sugar
1 lemon

Cut the melon flesh into cubes, removing all seeds. Put into a bowl with the sugar in layers and leave overnight. Put into a pan with a lemon cut in pieces and suspended in muslin. Simmer gently until the jam is golden and thick. Remove the lemon and pour jam into jars.

French Apricot Glazing Jelly

> 2½ lb ripe apricots
> 2 lb sugar

Remove the stones from the apricots and put the fruit through a mincer or nylon sieve. Mix the apricot purée and sugar carefully. Bring to the boil, stirring constantly. Boil without stirring for 15 minutes. Pour into small hot jars and cover.

Redcurrant Jelly with Wild Strawberries

> 3 lb redcurrants
> Sugar
> 8 oz wild strawberries

Heat the currants with ½ pint water and simmer until the fruit is pulped. Strain through a jelly bag. Measure the juice and allow 1 lb sugar to each pint of juice. Stir until the sugar has dissolved and boil rapidly to setting point. About 5 minutes before jelly is ready, add wild strawberries (or a few raspberries). Pour into small jars and cover.

Whitecurrant Bar-le-Duc

> 1 lb whitecurrants
> 12 oz cube sugar

Weigh the currants when they have been removed from their stems. Wash them well, drain, and put into a pan with the sugar. Cover and leave overnight. Bring to the boil very slowly, then boil for 3 minutes. Leave the currants with a cover on overnight. Pour into small jars and cover. The currants will be whole in a clear jelly.

CHAPTER SEVENTEEN
Candied Fruits, Crystallised Flowers and Fruit Pastes

Candied fruit and crystallised flowers are extremely expensive to buy, but they are interesting and comparatively inexpensive to make at home. Individual recipes are given, but a study of the general principles will enable the processing of a wide variety of fruit and flowers. Fruit pastes were sometimes known as 'leathers' since they resemble leather in texture. They provided a handy way of preserving a couple of centuries ago, and were much favoured as winter sweetmeats by American pioneers. They are still popular in Mediterranean countries and the Near East.

Candied Fruits

Candied or glacé fruits can be prepared from many fresh and canned fruits. When dried out in an oven, they are sometimes known as crystallised fruits, as when rolled and coated in sugar. Suitable fresh fruits are cherries, grapes, oranges and pears, pineapple and stone fruits. Canned apricots, pineapple, pears, mandarin oranges and lychees are also very good, and indeed process better than their fresh versions. The syrup should only be used for one type of fruit.

Good quality fresh fruit should be gently cooked in water until just tender before processing. Canned fruit should be drained from its syrup. Fresh fruit should be processed with a syrup made from ½ pint water and 6 oz sugar to each lb fruit. When using canned fruit, allow 1 lb fruit to ½ pint liquid made from the canning syrup and any necessary water.

Heat the syrup and use it to cover the fruit completely, keeping the fruit submerged with a saucer over the liquid if necessary. Leave to stand for 24 hours. Drain off the syrup, add 2 oz sugar and dissolve. Boil and pour over the fruit. Repeat this process twice more, adding 2 oz sugar each time. On the fifth day, add 3 oz sugar, and boil fruit for 4 minutes. Leave for 2 days. Repeat the process and leave the fruit to soak for

4 days. Drain off the syrup and put the fruit on a wire rack (such as a cake rack) to drain and finish off in a very cool oven or a warm airing cupboard for about 3 days. Store in boxes with waxed paper in a cool, dark dry place.

Good candied fruit should be firm outside with a succulent interior, of a bright colour and sweet but true fruit flavour. In the individual recipes in this chapter, these quantities may vary, as the methods have been gleaned from many sources, some of them very old, and it is worth experimenting to suit personal taste.

Crystallised Flowers

A variety of crystallised flowers can be made to use as cake decorations or small sweets. The flowers will last several months and keep their natural colours. Suitable flowers are primroses, violets, polyanthus, roses, carnation petals, forget-me-nots, mimosa, cowslips, sweet peas, fruit blossoms. Flowers which come from bulbs should not be eaten.

The flowers are crystallised in a solution of gum Arabic crystals and rose or orange flower water. Allow 3 teaspoons crystals to 3 tablespoons rose-water, and leave in a screwtop jar for two or three days, shaking sometimes, until the mixture is a sticky glue. A small soft paint brush is needed to paint the flowers. Large flowers should be taken apart and the petals re-assembled when needed. The petals must be completely coated, or bare spots will shrivel and not keep. A little vegetable colouring may be added to the solution, but this must be very delicate to remain natural. When the flowers have been sugared, they should be dried for about 24 hours until crisp and dry. They are best stored in the dark. For short-term use, flowers can be quickly crystallised with beaten egg white and sugar, but they will not store for long.

Fruit Pastes

Fruit pastes or leathers are made from fruit pulp cooked with an equal weight of sugar until the mixture is very dry and firm. It can be finished off in hot sun or in the oven and will store well between waxed paper in tins. An old recipe suggested that paste should be made from oranges, apples, cherries, pears and raspberries and should be moulded into small thin cakes. Before drying in the stove, they should be impressed with 'Wedgwood-ware seals, groups from the antique, etc. pressed upon them while still moist'.

Candied Angelica

> **Fresh angelica stems**
> **¼ oz salt**
> **4 pints water**
> **Sugar**

Cut stems from young plants in April, and cut them into 2–3 inch pieces. Cover with boiling brine in the proportion of ¼ oz salt to 4 pints water. Leave for 10 minutes and drain. Rinse in cold water. Put into boiling water and boil for 7 minutes until tender. Drain and scrape off the outer skin. Weigh the stems and allow an equal weight of sugar. For each lb sugar and lb angelica allow 1 pint water. Dissolve the sugar in the water, bring to the boil and pour over the stems. Leave for 24 hours. Bring to the boil again and take out the stems. Add 1 lb sugar to each original lb angelica again, and bring to the boil. Pour syrup over stems. Repeat this process for a total of 4 days. Leave stems to soak in syrup for 2 weeks. Drain the stems and leave on paper on a cooker rack to dry slowly.

Candied Apricots

   4 lb just-ripe apricots
   4 lb sugar
   1 pint water

Cut the skin carefully at the top of each apricot and squeeze out the stones. Make a syrup with sugar and water and when it starts to thicken, add the apricots and bring to the boil. Remove from heat, then bring to the boil again. Do this three more times, then pour fruit and syrup into a bowl and leave overnight. On the next day heat the syrup and fruit and boil for 1 minute. Drain the fruit and put into a bowl. Boil the syrup and pour over the fruit. Leave overnight. Repeat this process twice more until the apricots are saturated and the syrup has been absorbed. Place apricots on a rack covered with paper and dry in the sun or in an open oven, turning the fruit occasionally. When dry, store in a tin or wooden box.

Candied Cherries

   2 lb firm black cherries
   2 lb sugar
   1 pint water

The cherries should be weighed after stoning. Dissolve the sugar in the water over a low heat without boiling. When the syrup is clear, put in the cherries. Simmer very gently until the cherries are almost transparent. Drain the fruit and put on flat trays. Dry thoroughly in the sun or in a very cool oven with the door slightly open. Dust with icing sugar containing a pinch of bicarbonate of soda and store in a box with waxed paper layers.

Candied Chestnuts

> 2 lb chestnuts
> 2 lb sugar
> 1 vanilla pod
> 1 pint water

Remove outer casings from chestnuts and boil the nuts in water for 8 minutes. Remove the inner skin. Make a syrup with the sugar, water and vanilla pod, and when it is thick, put in the chestnuts and boil gently for 10 minutes. Remove the vanilla pod and pour nuts and syrup into a bowl and leave overnight. Reheat the syrup and chestnuts and boil for 1 minute, then pour back into the bowl and leave for 24 hours. Repeat the process three more times, until the syrup has been absorbed. Put the chestnuts on a wire rack covered with paper and dry them slowly in an open oven. Store in a wooden box lined with greaseproof paper and store in a cool dry place. Chestnuts tend to dry more quickly than other candied fruits and lose their flavour, so they should be eaten quickly.

Candied Figs

> 2 lb just-ripe figs
> 2 lb sugar
> 2 pints water

Prick the figs here and there with a needle. Make a syrup with the sugar and water and put into the figs. Boil for 10 minutes, pour into a bowl and leave overnight. On the next day, heat the syrup and fruit and boil for 1 minute. Drain the fruit and put into a bowl. Boil the syrup and pour over the fruit. Leave overnight. Repeat this process twice more until the figs are saturated and the syrup has been absorbed. Place figs on a rack covered with paper and dry in the sun or in an open oven, turning the fruit occasionally. When dry, store in a tin or wooden box. The figs will crystallise better the slower they are cooked and the more often they are put back in the syrup.

Candied Grapefruit Peel

Thin-skinned grapefruit
Sugar

Take the rinds from the grapefruit and cut into $\frac{1}{2}$ inch strips. Cover with cold water, bring to the boil and simmer for 5 minutes. Strain and return to the pan. Repeat process three times. In the final process, simmer the rinds until tender, strain and cover with cold water. Drain and weigh the rinds and weigh an equal quantity of sugar. Use the drained grapefruit liquid and make a syrup with the sugar. Simmer until syrup is clear, then add peel and boil until the syrup is thick. Drain the grapefruit peel on a wire rack in a very cool oven with the door open. Roll peel in granulated sugar with a pinch of bicarbonate of soda. The peel can also be dipped in melted plain chocolate to serve as a sweetmeat.

Candied Marrow

2 lb ripe marrow flesh
2 lb sugar
1 oz root ginger
10 cayenne pods
2 lemons

Cut the marrow into neat cubes. Cover with water and leave for 12 hours. Strain and mix with sugar and leave for 12 hours. Tie bruised root ginger, cayenne pods and the grated rind of the lemons into a muslin bag. Heat the marrow with the sugar and lemon juice until the sugar has dissolved. Put in the muslin bag, and simmer until the marrow is clear and the syrup is thick. Pour into a covered bowl and leave for 7 days.

Strain off the syrup and put marrow on waxed paper on a wire rack in a warm place to dry. Roll cubes in caster sugar containing a pinch of bicarbonate of soda and cream of tartar.

Candied Melon

1 just-ripe melon
1 pint water
1 dessertspoon white vinegar
Sugar

Peel the melon and remove pips. Cut the flesh into cubes and heat in water and vinegar. Bring to boiling point and take off heat. Bring to boil again and remove from heat. Repeat this process four more times, then cool and drain. Allow 2 lb sugar to 2 lb melon flesh and make into a syrup with 1 pint water. Bring to the boil and add melon cubes and boil for 10 minutes. Pour into a bowl and leave overnight. On the next day heat the syrup and fruit and boil for 1 minute. Drain the fruit and put into a bowl. Boil the syrup and pour over the fruit. Leave overnight. Repeat this process twice more until the melon cubes are saturated and the syrup has been absorbed. Place melon cubes on a rack covered with paper and dry in the sun or in an open oven, turning the fruit occasionally. When dry, store in a tin or wooden box.

Candied Oranges

6 medium oranges
Sugar

Make a small neat hole at the top of each orange and scoop out the pith and pulp with a small spoon. This pulp can be used for another preserve, or for ice cream, which could be used to fill the candied orange shells for a special occasion. Soak the orange skins in brine made from $\frac{1}{4}$ oz salt to 4 pints water for 7 days. Drain and soak the skins in fresh water for 3 days, changing the water each day. Make a syrup in the proportion of 1 lb sugar to 1 pint water, and boil the orange skins until they are clear. Drain and put on paper on a cooker rack until they lose their stickiness. Serve at the end of a meal on their own, or filled with ice cream or an orange mousse.

Candied Orange & Lemon Peel

Oranges
Lemons
Sugar

Remove the peel carefully from the fruit, if possible in quarters. Put the peel into a pan with enough water to cover and simmer for $1\frac{1}{2}$ hours, adding more water if necessary. Add 2 oz sugar for each fruit used and stir until dissolved. Bring to the boil, then put aside without a lid until the next day. On the next day, bring to the boil and simmer for 5 minutes. On the following day, simmer until the peel has absorbed nearly all the syrup. Drain the peel and put on paper on a cooker rack. Cover with greaseproof paper and dry slowly. A little syrup can be poured into the hollow of the peel pieces.

Candied Peaches

2 lb small peaches
2 lb sugar
1 pint water

Cut the peaches in half and remove stones and peel. Make a syrup with the sugar and water and bring to the boil. Add peaches and bring to the boil again. Remove from heat, then return to the boil. Do this three more times, then pour into a bowl and leave overnight. On the next day heat the syrup and fruit and boil for 1 minute. Drain the fruit and put into a bowl. Boil the syrup and pour over the fruit. Leave overnight. Repeat this process twice more until the peaches are saturated and the syrup has been absorbed. Place peaches on a rack covered with paper and dry in the sun or in an open oven, turning the fruit occasionally. When dry, store in a tin or wooden box.

Candied Pears

> 2 lb small just-ripe pears
> 2 lb sugar
> 1 pint water

Peel the pears but leave them whole with a small piece of stalk. Make up the syrup with sugar and water and bring to the boil. Add pears and bring to the boil again. Remove from heat, then return to the boil. Do this three more times, then pour into a bowl and leave overnight. On the next day heat the syrup and fruit and boil for 1 minute. Drain the fruit and put into a bowl. Boil the syrup and pour over the fruit. Leave overnight. Repeat this process twice more until the pears are saturated and the syrup has been absorbed. Place pears on a rack covered with paper and dry in the sun or in an open oven, turning the fruit occasionally. When dry, store in a tin or wooden box.

Candied Pineapple

> 2 lb just-ripe fresh pineapple
> 2 lb sugar
> 2 pints water

Cut the pineapple into small neat cubes. Make a syrup with the water and sugar. Add the pineapple and boil for 10 minutes. Pour into a bowl and leave overnight. On the next day heat the syrup and fruit and boil for

1 minute. Drain the fruit and put into a bowl. Boil the syrup and pour over the fruit. Leave overnight. Repeat this process twice more until the pineapple cubes are saturated and the syrup has been absorbed. Place pineapple on a rack covered with paper and dry in the sun or in an open oven, turning the fruit occasionally. When dry, store in a tin or wooden box.

Candied Plums

4 lb plums
4 lb sugar
4 pints water

Dissolve 2 lb sugar in 2 pints water and boil to 240°F (soft ball). Put firm ripe plums into a stone jar in this syrup. Cover and leave in a very cool oven overnight. Drain off the syrup and bring it to the boil. Pour over the plums in the jar and leave in the oven overnight. Repeat this process twice more, and drain plums. Make up some new syrup with remaining sugar and water, and boil to 240°F (soft ball). Put the plums into the new syrup, remove from heat and leave until cold. Drain the plums on to a wire rack and keep in a warm room until dry and firm. Store in a tin beween layers of waxed paper.

Candied Tangerines

2 lb very small tangerines
2 lb sugar
2 pints water

Soak the tangerines for 24 hours in cold water, changing the water several times. Make a syrup with the sugar and water and add the tangerines. Bring to the boil and boil for 10 minutes. Remove from heat, then bring to the boil again. Do this three more times, then pour fruit and syrup into a bowl and leave overnight. On the next day heat the syrup and fruit and boil for 1 minute. Drain the fruit and put into a bowl. Boil the syrup and pour over the fruit. Leave overnight. Repeat this process twice more until the tangerines are saturated and the syrup has been absorbed. Place tangerines on a rack covered with paper and dry in the sun or in an open oven, turning the fruit occasionally. When dry, store in a tin or wooden box.

Candied Tangerine Segments

2 lb tangerines
2 lb sugar
1 pint water

Use tangerines which are not too ripe. Peel and remove all white filaments from the segments. Take out pips with a large darning needle. Put the segments on a piece of paper and leave overnight. Make a syrup with the sugar and water. Add the segments and boil for 7 minutes. Remove from heat, then bring to the boil again. Do this three more times, then pour fruit and syrup into a bowl and leave overnight. On the next day heat the syrup and fruit and boil for 1 minute. Drain the fruit and put into a bowl. Boil the syrup and pour over the fruit. Leave overnight. Repeat this process twice more until the tangerines are saturated and the syrup has been absorbed. Place tangerines on a rack covered with paper and dry in the sun or in an open oven, turning the fruit occasionally. When dry, store in a tin or wooden box.

Candied Cowslips

10 oz yellow cowslip 'pips'
8 oz sugar

This recipe was first used in 1700. The flowers should be gathered when the dew is off, and only the yellow blossoms should be used. Dissolve the sugar in as little hot water as possible which will absorb the sugar (about 4 fluid oz). Bring to the boil and cook until the syrup starts to candy. Take off the heat and shake in the flowers gradually. Stir until the flowers become dry and sugary. Store in jars sealed with sticky tape.

Crystallised Mint Leaves

Fresh mint leaves
Egg white
Granulated sugar

Use fresh green mint and well-shaped leaves. Beat egg white stiffly and coat both sides of the leaves. Coat with sugar and put on a wire rack covered with wax paper. Stand on the rack of a cooker until dry. Store in a tin between layers of waxed paper. Use to garnish fruit cocktails and ice creams. This method may also be used for rose and carnation petals.

Crystallised Primroses

Primroses
Gum Arabic crystals (not powder)
Rose-water
Caster sugar

Take enough gum Arabic crystals to make the size of a walnut and put into a screwtop jar with 2 teaspoons rose-water. Leave overnight so that it dissolves. Use small quantities of fresh flowers, free from dust, dew or rain. Use a small soft paint brush to paint the gum Arabic solution on top and bottom of the petals thoroughly and evenly. Dredge lightly but thoroughly with caster sugar. Shake off surplus and put on to wire racks covered with sugared greaseproof paper. Dry on a cooker rack, or in an airing cupboard, or a very cool oven. The flowers should dry very slowly for 10–24 hours, so that they dry evenly and crisply. Store in tins layered with waxed paper.

Candied Roses and Violets

> 1 breakfastcup small rosebuds
> or 2 breakfastcups violets
> 8 oz granulated sugar
> 4 fluid oz water

This is a recipe from New Orleans, and the flowers are particularly suitable for decorating wedding or christening cakes. The flowers should be gathered early when the dew has just dried. Bring the water to the boil and remove from heat. Stir in the sugar until dissolved. Remove stems from the flowers, and lightly wash and drain them without bruising in a colander. Put the syrup back on the heat and stir in the flowers. Cook gently to 240°F (soft ball). Take off the heat and stir with a wooden spoon until the syrup begins to granulate to the texture of coarse meal. Pour the contents of the pan into a colander and shake off the extra sugar as the flowers cool. Store in jars with the lids sealed with sticky tape.

Apricot Paste

> Ripe apricots
> Sugar

Take stones from the apricots and cook them with as little water as possible to prevent sticking. Put through a fine sieve and weigh the pulp. Mix with an equal quantity of sugar and heat and stir until all the moisture has evaporated and the mixture is dry. Roll the paste on a sheet of paper sprinkled with caster sugar, and leave to dry in the sun or in an open oven. The paste should be leathery so that it can be rolled up.

Quince Paste

Quinces
Sugar
Icing sugar

Do not peel or core the quinces, but cut them into small pieces. Simmer in water just to cover until very soft. Sieve the pulp and take an equal weight of pulp and sugar. Put them into a thick pan and stir over a low heat until the mixture dries and leaves the sides of the pan clear. Cool slightly and then roll out $\frac{1}{2}$ inch thick on a board dusted with icing sugar. Stamp out rounds and leave them to dry, turning often until they are the texture of leather. Dust with icing sugar and store in tins. *Apple paste* and *pear paste* may be prepared in the same way. The mixture can be dried out on the rack of a cooker, or in a cool airing cupboard.

Redcurrant or Blackberry Paste

2 lb redcurrants or blackberries
Sugar
$\frac{1}{2}$ pint water

Heat the currants or berries in water until they burst and are soft. Drain through a jelly bag and weigh the juice. Take an equal quantity of sugar and heat slowly, stirring all the time until the mixture is thick and dry. Put the paste into a baking tin and sprinkle with caster sugar. When cold and hard, cut into pieces with a knife, dip in caster sugar and store in a wooden box lined with greaseproof paper.

CHAPTER EIGHTEEN
Jams for Sale or Competition

The competent jam-maker may want to enter competitions, and may also be interested in making jam for sale. To avoid disappointment in both areas, it is wise to study competition schedules and marking standards; and it is necessary to comply with Statutory Requirements for the labelling and sale of preserves.

Jam for Sale

Intending producers are recommended to study the official Ministry of Agriculture publication– Bulletin 21, Home Preservation of Fruit and Vegetables, which includes recipes for jams, jellies, marmalade, lemon curd and mincemeat. Preserves sold to the public must have a sufficiently high proportion of sugar to fruit (known as the soluble solid content), so that it is wise to follow the principles of preservation given in Bulletin 21. Recipes can be adapted, but under no circumstances should more than 10 lb of jam be obtained from 6 lb sugar, irrespective of the amount of fruit used. This is the finished weight when weighed in the pan and should result in nine full 1 lb pots for sale, with a little over.

Jars must be filled to the brim, and preferably covered with plastic tops put on correctly to ensure a vacuum seal. This means the preserve should be potted when near boiling, and each cover put on before the next pot is filled. Since lemon curd does not reach a sufficiently high temperature for the safe use of plastic tops, it should be covered with a waxed disc and cellulose cover. Methods of potting and covering are given in detail in Chapter One (EQUIPMENT, INGREDIENTS AND METHODS).

Jars should be cleaned of all stickiness, with neat and clearly written labels put on straight. The name of the jam should be included, and with jam made from mixed fruit, or with an unusual name, contents should be stated in descending order of bulk. The name and address of the maker should be included, sufficient to receive postal communications. The price should also be stated, and of course the weight. Jam, marmalade and jellies must be sold by net weight in amounts of 2 oz, 4 oz, 8 oz, 12 oz or 16 oz. Mincemeat and lemon curd must be sold by net weight, but not in prescribed amounts. As it is difficult to ensure a full 8 oz or 16 oz of these two preserves, the appropriate ½ lb and 1 lb jars should be marked 7 oz and 14 oz.

Jam for Competition

It is important to study a competition schedule thoroughly before preparing an entry. If rules are not complied with, an entry can be discarded before judging takes place.

Marks are usually given for appearance and presentation of jam and container; colour; condition; consistency; flavour; originality (in open classes).

Jars should be filled right to the top and correctly covered with a wax disc and top covering suitable to the preserve. The jar should also be suitable to the preserve, free from blemish and showing no brand name of previous contents. Labels should be neatly written or printed, and put on straight, level with the base of the jar or parallel to it. Jars which are well-polished show the colour of the jam to best advantage. The importance of correct covering cannot be over-emphasised (see Chapter One, EQUIPMENT, INGREDIENTS AND METHODS) as this will affect not only appearance but also condition of the preserve. Points are soon lost if jams have faint signs of mould, are sugary or taste fermented.

The colour of the jam should be bright, and jellies must be completely clear. Whole fruit should be well distributed, and a jam must be firm but not over-stiff. Jelly should be firm but not hard, sticky or syrupy. Jam and jellies should taste and smell like fresh fruit, with a well-balanced proportion of ingredients when mixed fruits are used. The taste of fruit skins or peels is important, and these should never be tough.

The originality of a recipe will add extra points in an open class. If a curd is entered, the jar should be full to the brim (lemon curd shrinks) and covered while hot. A fruit curd should be smooth with a fresh flavour, and the jars must also be well-filled. Fruit cheese should be shown in a shallow, straight or sloping sided jar, and should have a fruity flavour. Fruit butter should come within $\frac{1}{2}$ inch of the jar top, and have an airtight seal, not a wax circle; it must spread and be of an even colour.

Recipe Index